teenytiny
crochet

D1119531

teenytiny crochet

35 adorably small projects

Catherine Hirst

CICO BOOKS

LONDON NEW YORK

Published in 2012 by CICO Books
An imprint of
Ryland Peters & Small Ltd
519 Broadway, 5th floor
New York, NY 10012

www.cicobooks.com

10 9 8 7 6 5 4 3 2 1

Text © Catherine Hirst 2012
Design and photography ©
CICO Books 2012

The author's moral rights have been
asserted. All rights reserved. No
part of this publication may be
reproduced, stored in a retrieval
system, or transmitted in any form
or by any means, electronic,
mechanical, photocopying, or
otherwise, without the prior
permission of the publisher.

A CIP catalog record for this book
is available from the Library of
Congress.

ISBN 978 1 908170 47 7

Printed in China

Managing Editor: Gillian Haslam
Editor: Marie Clayton
Pattern checker: Susan Horan
Design concept: Luis Peral Aranda
Designer: Elizabeth Healey
Photographer: Geoff Dann
Room sets designed and made by
Trina Dalziel

For digital editions visit
www.cicobooks.com/apps.php

Contents

CHAPTER 1

Flying friends

CHAPTER 2

Furry friends

CHAPTER 3

Home sweet home

CHAPTER 4

Pretty things

CHAPTER 5

Tiny friends

Introduction

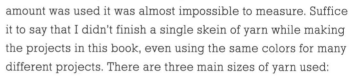

I have always loved small things. When I was a little girl, my uncle made me a dolls' house, and I spent many happy hours rearranging the furniture and dolls that lived inside, making up stories about their lives. So to create these projects in miniature was a labor of love for me! The projects in this book are meant to inspire the imagination in the same way—from Gus the dachshund chasing lizards on the farm where he lives, to the Russian doll sisters living in their onion dome in St Petersburg. Children will love playing with these pieces and creating their lives, and many of the projects make lovely gifts for the young or young-at-heart! Don't give them to babies or very small children though, because many items are tiny enough to swallow.

The very tiny crochet hooks used for the projects are steel hooks, which come in smaller sizes than aluminum hooks. If you've never used small hooks and thin crochet cotton, it may take some patience until it feels natural. Try to loosen your tension—if you make tiny stitches too tight, you won't be able to insert your hook.

Many projects do not have exact yarn amounts specified because such a tiny

amount was used it was almost impossible to measure. Suffice it to say that I didn't finish a single skein of yarn while making the projects in this book, even using the same colors for many different projects. There are three main sizes of yarn used:

- **No.8 crochet cotton**: this is the thinnest yarn used (the larger the number, the thinner the yarn), for the very tiny pieces and requires some getting used to. A few projects are crocheted with embroidery thread, which is about the same thickness.
- **No.5 crochet cotton**: I used this for the majority of the projects; it's a manageable size and because most crochet cotton is mercerized and so slightly shiny, it gives a lovely sheen to the projects and makes them look very neat. I can highly recommend DMC Petra No.5 cotton, which is lovely and silky to work with.
- **Baby (fingering) yarn and sock yarn**: these are used with a smaller hook than usual to make the tight stitches needed. Throughout the book I have given the yarn weight allowing you to make substitutions. You can scale these projects up by using a larger yarn and hook if desired, but remember to use a smaller hook than usual for the yarn for a tight tension.

Stuff the projects firmly, but do not overstuff or you will pull the stitches apart and the stuffing will show through. Crochet cotton is much easier to stuff firmly because cotton is not

elastic so the stitches will not tend to stretch as much; be more careful about overstuffing when you are using either the fingering yarn or the sock yarn.

Most of the projects in this book are made using the spiral method, so the ends of rounds are not joined with a slip stitch. Use a stitch marker to mark the first stitch of each round—I used a very small safety pin slipped through the stitch because a larger stitch marker would get in the way. Any projects not made with the spiral method are clearly noted in the pattern, including the slip stitch and chain 1 needed for the joined method. Almost all the projects start with a magic circle. This method of beginning a 3-D crochet project is brilliant because it results in no hole whatsoever in the top of the piece. If you've never used the magic circle method before, you can find clear instructions in the Basic Techniques section on page 119. You could also look online for video tutorials of the technique.

Using safety eyes or embroidering eyes is essential if you are giving the item to a young child. If the recipient is an adult (or yourself!) you can insert the safety eyes at the end without putting on the backs—they will stay in place once inserted.

I had a wonderful time creating these projects and I know you will too. Happy crocheting!

CHAPTER 1

Flying friends

From the tiniest ducks you have ever seen to wee owls, robins, and butterflies, this chapter is all about our sweet winged friends. Why not make a pair of lovebirds to show someone you really care? Or perch some robins on your kitchen windowsill to remind you that spring is just around the corner? There's even a nest pattern included so your flying friends can have their own little home.

Mama and Baby Bird

Mama Fuzzy Bird spoils her Baby Bird; she feeds him only the very choicest worms, and makes sure their nest is always clean, cozy, and warm. She likes to snuggle up to his fuzzy little head at night and tell him long stories about all the creatures who live in their forest. Baby Bird can't wait to explore the big, wide world.

MAMA BIRD

BODY

Make 6sc in magic circle, pull tail to close.

Rnd 1: 2sc in each sc. (12 sts)

Rnd 2: *1sc in next sc, 2sc in next sc; rep from * to end. (18 sts)

Rnd 3: *1sc in each of next 2 sc, 2sc in next sc; rep from * to end. (24 sts)

Rnd 4: *1sc in each of next 3 sc, 2sc in next sc; rep from * to end. (30 sts)

Rnd 5: *1sc in each of next 4 sc, 2sc in next sc; rep from * to end. (36 sts)

Rnds 6–11: 1sc in each sc. (36 sts)

Rnd 12: *1sc in each of next 4 sc, sc2tog; rep from * to end. (30 sts)

Rnd 13: *1sc in each of next 3 sc, sc2tog; rep from * to end. (24 sts)

Rnd 14: *1sc in each of next 2 sc, sc2tog; rep from * to end. (18 sts)

Rnd 15: *1sc in next sc, sc2tog; rep from * to end. (12 sts)

  Turn inside out. Attach safety eyes. Stuff firmly.

Rnd 16: Sc2tog around. (6 sts)

  Fasten off, leaving a long tail. Weave through rem sts and pull tight to close.

WINGS (MAKE 2)

Make 6sc in magic circle, pull tail to close.

Rnd 1: 2sc in each sc. (12 sts)

Rnd 2: 2sc in each sc. (24 sts)

Rnd 3: *1sc in next sc, 2sc in next sc; rep from * to end. (36 sts)

  Fasten off, leaving a long tail.

Notes: Use one strand of each yarn held together throughout—both birds were made with less than one ball of each. After making each piece, turn inside out—the reverse side will be fuzzier. You will need to turn the main body inside out before making the final decreases.

SIZES

Mama bird: 1½ in. long

Baby bird: 1 in. long

Nest: 2⅛ in. diameter

ABBREVIATIONS

rem: remaining

rep: repeat

Rnd(s): round, rounds

sc: single crochet

sc2tog: single crochet 2 together decrease. Insert hook in next st, yo, pull through a loop. Without finishing st, insert hook in next st, yo and pull through a loop. Yo and pull through all three loops on hook

ss: slip stitch

st(s): stitch, stitches

yo: yarn over hook

MATERIALS

Birds

- ⅛ x ball, approx 22 yds, of No.8 crochet cotton, such as Rubi Perle No.8 100% cotton, in pale green
- ⅛ x ball, approx 28½ yds, of laceweight yarn, such Rowan Kidsilk Haze 70% mohair/30% silk in pale green
- 1.5mm (size 8) steel crochet hook
- 2 x pairs ¼ in. (6mm) safety eyes
- Toy stuffing
- Sewing needle
- Small piece orange felt
- Fabric/craft adhesive

Nest

- ⅛ x 50g ball, approx 28½ yds, of No.5 crochet cotton, such as Anchor Artiste No.5 100% cotton, in beige
- 2.0mm (size 4) steel crochet hook

Make me a cozy nest to sit in!

BABY BIRD

BODY

Make 6sc in magic circle, pull tail to close.

Rnd 1: 2sc in each sc. (12 sts)

Rnd 2: *1sc in next sc, 2sc in next sc; rep from * to end. (18 sts)

Rnd 3: *1sc in each of next 2 sc, 2sc in next sc; rep from * to end. (24 sts)

Rnds 4–9: 1sc in each sc. (24 sts)

Rnd 10: *1sc in each of next 2 sc, sc2tog; rep from * to end. (18 sts)

Rnd 11: *1sc in next sc, sc2tog; rep from * to end. (12 sts)

Turn inside out. Attach safety eyes. Stuff firmly.

Rnd 12: Sc2tog around. (6 sts)

Fasten off, leaving a long tail. Weave through rem sts and pull tight to close.

WINGS (MAKE 2)

Make 6sc in magic circle, pull tail to close.

Rnd 1: 2sc in each sc. (12 sts)

Rnd 2: 2sc in each sc. (24 sts)

Fasten off, leaving a long tail.

FINISHING

Fold each wing in half to make a half-moon shape. Sew flat side of each wing to either side of body. Cut a triangle of orange felt for beak and attach with fabric/craft adhesive.

BIRD'S NEST

Make 6sc in magic circle, pull tail to close.

Rnd 1: 2sc in each sc. (12 sts)

Rnd 2: *1sc in next sc, 2sc in next sc; rep from * around. (18 sts)

Rnd 3: *1sc in each of next 2 sc, 2sc in next sc; rep from * around. (24 sts)

Rnd 4: *1sc in each of next 3 sc, 2sc in next sc; rep from * around. (30 sts)

Rnd 5: *1sc in each of next 4 sc, 2sc in next sc; rep from * around. (36 sts)

Rnd 6: *1sc in each of next 5 sc, 2sc in next sc; rep from * around. (42 sts)

Rnd 7: *1sc in each of next 6 sc, 2sc in next sc; rep from * around. (48 sts)

Rnd 8: *1sc in each of next 7 sc, 2sc in next sc; rep from * around. (54 sts)

Rnds 9–13: 1sc in each sc. (54 sts)

Ss in next st, fasten off.

FINISHING

Weave in ends.

Notes: Both the birds and the nest are made in continuous spiral rounds, so you will not join with a slip stitch. Use a stitch marker to mark the first stitch of each round throughout. You could also use the nest pattern to make a tiny bowl to hold earrings on your dressing table, or coins on your bookshelf.

Wise Little Owls

Twit twoo! These two little owls, Sunshine and Snowy, have such big eyes because they go hunting for tasty mice late at night when all the other birds are asleep. They are very wise and like to read histories and adventure stories.

SIZE

1¼ in. tall

ABBREVIATIONS

ch: chain
dc: double crochet
hdc: half double crochet
rep: repeat
Rnd(s): round, rounds
sc: single crochet
ss: slip stitch
st(s): stitch, stitches

MATERIALS

- Oddments of No.5 crochet cotton, such as DMC Petra No.5 100% cotton, in white or yellow
- 1.5mm (size 8) steel crochet hook
- Cream or yellow felt
- 1 x pair safety eyes for each owl
- Sewing needle
- Toy stuffing
- Orange felt
- Craft/fabric adhesive

OWL

Make 6sc in magic circle; pull tail to close circle.

Rnd 1: 2sc in each sc. (12 sts)

Rnd 2: *1sc in next sc, 2sc in next sc; rep from * to end. (18 sts)

Rnd 3: *1sc in each of next 2 sc, 2sc in next sc; rep from * to end. (24 sts)

Rnds 4–11: 1sc in each sc. (24 sts)

Fasten off.

You could make me a nest too–see the pattern on page 12.

WINGS (MAKE 2)

Make 5sc in magic circle. Pull tail to make half-moon shape.

Row 1: Ch1, 1sc in each sc across.

Fasten off, leaving a long tail.

FINISHING

Cut two circles of cream or yellow felt, push a safety eye through the center of each and attach to head. Stitch edges of felt circles in place with running st.

Stuff owl. Press two halves of open top of owl together so eyes are at front. Join yarn to sc at side, work ears and join both thicknesses: 3ch, 1dc in next st, 1hdc in next st, 1sc in each of next 2 sts, ss in each of next 2 sts, 1sc in each of next 2 sts, 1hdc in next st, 1dc in each of last 2 sts.

Fasten off.

Sew flat side of wings to sides of body.

Cut a small triangle from orange felt and stick below eyes for beak.

Beautiful Butterflies

Colorful butterflies flit from flower to flower, looking so lovely... these little gems can be made into hair ornaments, used to adorn a garment, or even attached to a rod and inserted into the soil of a houseplant. The only limit is your imagination!

Have you seen any good flowers lately?

BUTTERFLY WINGS (MAKE 2 FOR EACH BUTTERFLY)

Using B, ch8, ss in first ch to form lp for lower wing.

Rnd 1: Ch12, ss in first ch to form lp for upper wing.

Rnd 2: Ch1, 10sc in lower wing lp, ss between lps, 14sc in upper wing lp, join with ss in first sc.

Fasten off.

Using C, join into any sc.

Rnd 3: *1sc in first sc, 2sc in next sc; rep from * around, while slip stitching in ss. Ss in first sc to close. (36 sc)

Rnd 4: Ss in each of next 3 sc, *ch2, ss in same sc as last ss (picot made), ss in each of next 2 sc; rep from * 12 times, ch2, ss in same sc as last ss, ss in each of last 6 sc, join with ss in first ss.

Fasten off.

FINISHING

Place two flat edges of wings together. Join A to first ss after last picot on lower wing, working through both pieces, work sc down flat edges to first picot on upper wing (for tail), ch4 (for head), skip first ch, sc in next 3 ch. 1sc in each sc of joining row, then ch4 (for tail), skip first ch, ss in next 3 ch, ss in each sc to last 3 sc.

Fasten off.

Cut a length of A and pull through top of butterfly head with hook to form antennae; make a knot in each end, then trim just above knot.

FLOWER

Ch4, join with ss to form ring.

Rnd 1: Ch3, 11dc in ring, join with ss in top of first ch-3.

Rnd 2: Ch1, *ch4, skip next dc, 1sc in next dc; rep from * ending 4ch, skip last dc, ss in first ch to join.

Rnd 3: *Ss in next ch-4 sp, [ch3, 3dc, ch3, ss] all in same sp; rep from * to end.

Fasten off.

FINISHING

Weave in ends.

SIZES

Butterfly: 1¼ in. long
Flower: 1¾ in. diameter

ABBREVIATIONS

ch(s): chain, chains
dc: double crochet
lp(s): loop; loops
rep: repeat
Rnd(s): round, rounds
sc: single crochet
sp: space
ss: slip stitch
st(s): stitch, stitches

MATERIALS

Butterflies
- Small amounts of No.5 crochet cotton, such as DMC Petra No.5 100% cotton, in green (A)
- Oddments of No.5 crochet cotton, such as DMC Petra No.5 100% cotton, in at least two other colors (B) and (C)
- 1.5mm (size 8) steel crochet hook

Flowers
- Small amount of 4-ply baby yarn, such as Patons Fairytale Dreamtime 4-ply 100% wool, in various colors
- 2.0mm (size 4) steel crochet hook

Robin Red Breast

When the robins start building their nests in the garden, spring has definitely arrived! With their distinctive red breasts, these tiny robins will make you smile—make a whole family to brighten up your life. And everyone needs a cozy home, so why not make the little nest as well to hold the robin family?

Spring has sprung, time to find a good place to build a nest.

ROBIN

BODY

Using A, make 6sc in magic circle, pull tail to close.

Rnd 1: 2sc in each sc. (12 sts)

Rnd 2: *1sc in next sc, 2sc in next sc; rep from * to end. (18 sts)

Rnds 3–6: 1sc in each sc. (18 sts)

Rnd 7: *1sc in next sc, sc2tog; rep from * to end. (12 sts)

   Insert safety eyes and secure. Stuff firmly.

Rnd 8: Sc2tog around. (6 sts)

   Fasten off, leaving a long tail.

RED BREAST

Using B, make 6sc in magic circle, pull tail to close.

Rnd 1: 2sc in each sc. (12 sts)

Rnd 2: *1sc in next sc, 2 sc in next sc; rep from * to end. (18 sts)

   Ss in next stitch, fasten off, leaving a long tail.

WINGS (MAKE 2)

In magic circle, ch2 and make 5hdc; pull tail to half-moon shape.

   Fasten off, leaving a long tail.

SIZES

Robin: 1¼ in. tall, 1½ in. across

Nest: 2¾ in. diameter

ABBREVIATIONS

ch(s): chain, chains

dc: double crochet

hdc: half double crochet

rep: repeat

Rnd(s): round, rounds

sc: single crochet

sc2tog: single crochet 2 together decrease. Insert hook in next st, yo, pull through a loop. Without finishing st, insert hook in next st, yo and pull through a loop. Yo and pull through all three loops on hook

ss: slip stitch

st(s): stitch, stitches

yo: yarn over hook

MATERIALS

Robin

• Small amount of DK weight pure wool in beige (A) and red (B)

• 3.5mm (size 00) steel crochet hook

• 1 x pair ¼ in. (6mm) safety eyes

• Toy stuffing

• Sewing needle

• Small piece of orange felt

• Craft/fabric adhesive

Nest

• ¼ x 50g ball, approx 28½ yds, of DK weight pure wool in beige (A)

• 2.5mm (size 2) steel crochet hook

• Sewing needle

Note: The nest is made in continuous spiral rounds, so you will not join with a slip stitch. Use a stitch marker throughout to mark the first stitch of each round.

TAIL

Ch5, [4dc, ss] in fourth ch from hook, ss in next ch, ch3, [4dc, ss] in same ch.
  Fasten off, leaving a long tail.

FINISHING

Use yarn end to sew hole in body closed.
  Sew breast, wings and tail to body using yarn ends.
  Cut a small triangle of orange felt for the beak and stick below eyes.

BIRD'S NEST

Make 6sc in magic circle, pull tail to close.

Rnd 1: 2sc in each sc. (12 sts)

Rnd 2: *1sc in next sc, 2sc in next sc; rep from * around. (18 sts)

Rnd 3: *1sc in each of next 2 sc, 2sc in next sc; rep from * around. (24 sts)

Rnd 4: *1sc in each of next 3 sc, 2sc in next sc; rep from * around. (30 sts)

Rnd 5: *1sc in each of next 4 sc, 2sc in next sc; rep from * around. (36 sts)

Rnd 6: *1sc in each of next 5 sc, 2sc in next sc; rep from * around. (42 sts)

Rnd 7: *1sc in each of next 6 sc, 2sc in next sc; rep from * around. (48 sts)

Rnd 8: *1sc in each of next 7 sc, 2sc in next sc; rep from * around. (54 sts)

Rnds 9–13: 1sc in each sc. (54 sts)
  Ss in next st, fasten off.

FINISHING

Weave in ends.

Teeny Ducks on a Pond

Quack! Matilda, Stella, and Bonnie are three ducks who all live together in a small pond. They eat lots of algae, insects and small fish and sometimes they find a particularly choice frog. They spend the rest of their time quacking to each other about their ducklings and all the goings-on in the pond.

DUCK
BODY

Using A and 1.4mm (size 9) hook, make 6sc in magic circle, pull tail to close.

Rnd 1: 2sc in each sc. (12 sts)

Rnd 2: *1sc in next sc, 2sc in next sc; rep from * to end. (18 sts)

Rnds 3–5: 1sc in each of next 3 sts, 1hdc in each of next 2 sts, 1dc in each of next 2 sts, 1hdc in each of next 2 sts, 1sc in each of next 3 sts, 1hdc in next st, 1dc in each of next 2 sts, 1hdc in next st, 1sc in each of next 2 sts. (18 sts)

Rnd 6: 1sc in each of next 3 sts, hdc2tog, dc2tog, hdc2tog, sc in each of next 9 sts. (15 sts)

Stuff firmly.

Rnd 7: 1sc in each of next 3 sts, [sc2tog] 3 times, 1sc in next st, [sc2tog] twice, 1sc in next st. (10 sts)

Ss in next st. Fasten off, leaving a long tail.

SIZES
Ducks: ⅞ in. long
Pond: 1¾ in. diameter

ABBREVIATIONS
dc: double crochet
dc2tog: double crochet 2 together decrease. *Yo, insert hook into first st, yo, pull through a loop, yo and pull yarn through first two loops on hook. Without finishing st, rep from * into next st. Yo and pull yarn through all three loops on hook

hdc: half double crochet
hdc2tog: half double crochet 2 together decrease. *Yo, insert hook into first st, yo, pull through a loop. Without finishing st, rep from * into next st. Yo and pull yarn through all five loops on hook
rep: repeat
Rnd(s): round, rounds
sc: single crochet
sc2tog: single crochet 2 together decrease. Insert hook in next st, yo, pull through a loop. Without finishing st, insert hook in next st, yo and pull through a loop. Yo and pull through all three loops on hook
ss: slip stitch
st(s): stitch, stitches
yo: yarn over hook

MATERIALS
Ducks
• ¼ x ball, approx 11 yds, of No.8 crochet cotton, such as Rubi Perle No.8 100% cotton, in yellow (A)
• 1.4mm (size 9) steel crochet hook
• Oddment of 6-strand embroidery floss in orange, split into 3 strands (B)
• Oddment of 6-strand embroidery floss in black
• Toy stuffing
• Sewing needle

Pond
• Small amount of No.5 crochet cotton, such as DMC Petra No.5 100% cotton, in blue (C)
• 1.5mm (size 8) steel crochet hook

Where's the pond, Matilda?

DUCK HEAD

Using A and 1.4mm (size 9) hook, make 6sc in magic circle, pull tail to close.

Rnd 1: 2sc in each sc. (12 sts)

Rnds 2–4: 1sc in each sc. (12 sts)

Stuff head.

Rnd 5: Sc2tog around. (6 sts)

Fasten off, leaving a long tail.

BEAK

Using B and 1.4mm (size 9) hook, make 6sc in magic circle. Pull tail to make half-moon shape.

FINISHING

Use yarn end to close hole in duck body. Use yarn end to sew head to body. Sew flat side of beak to head. Embroider eyes on either side of head using black embroidery floss.

POND

Using C and 1.5mm (size 8) hook, make 6sc in magic circle, pull tail to close.

Rnd 1: 2sc in each sc. (12 sts)

Rnd 2: *1sc in next sc, 2sc in next sc; rep from * to end. (18 sts)

Rnd 3: *1sc in each of next 2 sc, 2sc in next sc; rep from * to end. (24 sts)

Rnd 4: *1sc in each of next 3 sc, 2sc in next sc; rep from * to end. (30 sts)

Rnd 5: *1sc in each of next 4 sc, 2sc in next sc; rep from * to end. (36 sts)

Rnd 6: *1sc in each of next 5 sc, 2sc in next sc; rep from * to end. (42 sts)

Rnd 7: *1sc in each of next 6 sc, 2sc in next sc; rep from * to end. (48 sts)

Rnd 8: Ss in next st, *ch3, skip 1 st, ss in next st; rep from * to end.

Fasten off.

FINISHING

Weave in ends.

Lovable Lovebirds

Little birds in love: is there anything sweeter? These tiny lovebirds could be used stand-alone, or attached to hair ornaments, used as buttons, or why not thread a ribbon through the top and hang them from a miniature tree or potted plant? Wherever you use them, they will bring a little love and happiness.

Lovebirds make the world go round.

LOVEBIRD

Make 6sc in magic circle; pull tail to close.

Rnd 1: 2sc in each sc. (12 sts)

Rnd 2: *1sc in next sc, 2sc in next sc; rep from * to end. (18 sts)

Rnd 3: *1sc in each of next 2 sc, 2sc in next sc; rep from * to end. (24 sts)

Rnds 4–8: 1sc in each sc. (24 sts)

Rnd 9: *1sc in each of next 2 sc, sc2tog; rep from * to end. (18 sts)

Rnd 10: *1sc in next sc, sc2tog; rep from * to end. (12 sts)

Stuff lightly and flatten sphere to disc shape.

Rnd 11: Sc2tog around. (6 sts)

Fasten off, leaving a long tail.

FINISHING

Use yarn end to close hole in lovebird.

Cut two heart shapes from red felt and attach one on each side as wings using adhesive. Cut diamond shape from orange felt, fold in half and sew to front of disc for beak.

Embroider eyes using 3 strands of the black embroidery floss.

SIZE

1 in. diameter

ABBREVIATIONS

rep: repeat

Rnd(s): round, rounds

sc: single crochet

sc2tog: single crochet 2 together decrease. Insert hook in next st, yo, pull through a loop. Without finishing st, insert hook in next st, yo and pull through a loop. Yo and pull through all three loops on hook

st(s): stitch, stitches

yo: yarn over hook

MATERIALS

- Small amount of No.5 crochet cotton, such as DMC Petra No.5 100% cotton, in white
- 1.5mm (size 8) steel crochet hook
- Toy stuffing
- Sewing needle
- Small pieces of red and orange felt
- Oddment of 6-strand cotton embroidery floss in black, split into 3 strands
- Craft/fabric adhesive

CHAPTER 2

Furry friends

Everybody loves little animals... and there's a project just for you in this chapter, whether your furry favorite is a dog, a cat, or even a fuzzy sheep. You can have fun making the accessories that really make the projects complete—apples for the little piggies, the fish for Harry the cat, and of course a tasty bone for Gus the wiener dog!

The Three Bears

Mama Bear wants to make sure her family is warm and cozy during their long hibernation, so she's spent winter evenings crocheting blankets for all three of them. This pattern requires less sewing up because the head and body of the bear are made in one piece.

SIZES
Papa/Mama bears: 3¾ in. tall
Baby bear: 2 in. tall
Striped blanket: 2⅛ x 2 in.
Rose square blanket: 2 x 2 in.
Granny square blanket: 1¾ x 1¾ in.

ABBREVIATIONS
beg: beginning
ch: chain
cont: continue
dc: double crochet
hdc: half double crochet
rem: remaining
rep: repeat
Rnd(s): round, rounds
sc: single crochet
sc2tog: single crochet 2 together decrease. Insert hook in next st, yo, pull through a loop. Without finishing st, insert hook in next st, yo and pull through a loop. Yo and pull through all three loops on hook
sp: space
ss: slip stitch
st(s): stitch, stitches
yo: yarn over hook

MATERIALS
Papa Teddy Bear
• ⅒ x ball, approx 45 yds, of 4-ply cotton yarn, such as Patons 4-ply 100% cotton, in green (MC)
• Small amount of 4-ply wool, such as Patons Fairytale Dreamtime 4-ply 100% wool, in blue (CC)
• 2.0mm (size 4) steel crochet hook

Mama Teddy Bear
• ⅒ x ball, approx 37 yds, of 4-ply cotton yarn, such as Wendy Supreme 4-ply 100% cotton, in pink (MC)
• Small amount of 4-ply wool, such as Patons Fairytale Dreamtime 4-ply 100% wool, in pink (CC)
• 2.0mm (size 4) steel crochet hook

Baby Teddy Bear
• Small amount of No.8 crochet cotton, such as DMC Cotton Perle No.8 100% cotton, in purple (MC)
• Small amount of No.8 crochet cotton, such as Rubi Perle No.8 100% cotton, in cream (CC)
• 1.4mm (size 9) steel crochet hook

All bears
• Toy stuffing
• Embroidery floss in red and blue
• Sewing needle

Striped and Granny Square Blankets
• Oddments of No.8 crochet cotton, such as Rubi Perle No.8 100% cotton, in various colors
• 1.5mm (size 8) steel crochet hook
• Yarn needle

Rose Square Blanket
• Oddments of No.8 crochet cotton, such as Rubi Perle No.8 100% cotton, in pink (A) and cream (B)
• 1.4mm steel (size 9) crochet hook
• Yarn needle

BEAR

HEAD/BODY

Using MC, make 6sc in magic circle and pull tail to close.

Rnd 1: 2sc in each sc. (12 sts)

Rnd 2: *1sc in next sc, 2sc in next sc; rep from * to end. (18 sts)

Rnd 3: *1sc in each of next 2 sc, 2sc in next sc; rep from * to end. (24 sts)

Rnd 4: *1sc in each of next 3 sc, 2sc in next sc; rep from * to end. (30 sts)

Rnd 5: 1sc in each sc. (30 sts)

Rnd 6: *1sc in each of next 3 sc, sc2tog; rep from * to end. (24 sts)

Rnd 7: *1sc in each of next 2 sc, sc2tog; rep from * to end. (18 sts)

Rnd 8: *1sc in next sc, sc2tog; rep from * to end. (12 sts)

Stuff firmly.

Rnd 9: Sc2tog around. (6 sts)

Begin making body:

Rnd 10: 2sc in each sc. (12 sts)

Rnd 11: *1sc in next sc, 2sc in next sc; rep from * to end. (18 sts)

Rnd 12: *1sc in each of next 2 sc, 2sc in next sc; rep from * to end. (24 sts)

Rnds 13–16: 1 sc in each sc. (24 sts)

Rnd 17: *1sc in each of next 2 sc, sc2tog; rep from * to end. (18 sts)

Rnd 18: *1sc in next sc, sc2tog; rep from * to end. (12 sts)

Stuff firmly. If more stuffing in head is desired, use non-hook end of a larger crochet hook to push stuffing up into head.

Rnd 19: Sc2tog around. (6 sts)

Cut yarn, leaving a long tail. Thread through rem sts and pull tight to close.

EARS (MAKE 2)

Using MC, make 6sc in magic circle. Pull tail to make half circle.

Fasten off, leaving a tail for sewing.

ARMS (MAKE 2)

Using MC, make 6sc in magic circle and pull tail to close.

Rnd 1: *1sc in next sc, 2sc in next sc; rep from * to end. (9 sts)

Rnd 2: 1sc in each sc. (9 sts)

Rnd 3: *1sc in next sc, sc2tog; rep from * to end. (6 sts)

Cont making 1sc in each sc (no need to use a stitch marker) until arms are desired length (teddies shown have 3 rounds). When desired length is reached, ss in next st, then fasten off, leaving a long tail.

LEGS (MAKE 2)

Using CC, make 8sc in magic circle and pull tail to close.

Rnd 1: *1sc in next sc, 2sc in next sc; rep from * to end. (12 sts)

Change to MC.

Rnd 2: 1sc in each sc. (12 sts)

Rnd 3: *1sc in next sc, sc2tog; rep from * to end. (8 sts)

Cont making 1sc in each sc (no need to use a stitch marker) until legs are desired length (teddies shown have 3 rounds). When desired length is reached, ss in next st, then finish off, leaving a long tail.

Who's been sleeping in my bed?

Notes:
All bears are made with the same pattern; Baby Bear is made with a smaller hook and finer yarn to make him smaller overall. If you want to use safety eyes, add them before stuffing the head.

FINISHING

Sew ears to head with flat side facing head. Curl slightly toward front of face. Stuff arms and legs if desired (tail of yarn can be stuffed inside and used as padding).

Sew arms and legs to body.

Embroider nose and mouth using red embroidery floss. Embroider French knots in blue embroidery floss for eyes.

BLANKETS

STRIPED BLANKET FOR PAPA TEDDY BEAR

Change color every other row throughout.

Using 1.5mm (size 8) hook, ch 21.

Row 1: Skip first ch, 1sc in each sc, turn. (20 sts)

Row 2: 1sc in each sc, turn.

Rep Row 2 another 20 times.

To make border, attach new color and sc in each sc, making 16 sc down each side, ch1 before turning each corner.

Fasten off, weave in all ends.

> Note: The bear head and body are made in one piece in continuous spiral rounds, so you will not join with a slip stitch. Use a stitch marker throughout to mark the first stitch of each round.

ROSE SQUARE BLANKET FOR MAMA TEDDY BEAR (MAKE 4 SQUARES)

Using A and 1.4mm (size 9) hook, ch4, join with ss to form a ring.

Rnd 1: 8sc in ring.

Rnd 2: *ch4, skip 1 sc, 1sc in next sc; rep from * to end, ss in base of first ch-4 to join.

Rnd 3: *ss in next ch-4 sp, [1sc, 1hdc, 1sc] in same sp; rep from * to end.

Rnd 4: *ss between two petals, ch6; rep from * to end, ss in first ss to join.

Change to B.

Rnd 5: Join in any ch-6 sp and ch3, [2dc, ch2, 3dc] in same sp, ch1. *In next ch-6 sp, [3dc, ch2, 3dc], ch 1. Rep from * to end; ss in top of first ch-3 to join.

Using A, join squares with sc.

Using A, sc around edge of entire blanket.

Fasten off, weave in ends.

GRANNY SQUARE BLANKET FOR BABY TEDDY BEAR (MAKE 4 SQUARES)

Change color each round.

Using 1.5mm (size 8) hook, ch4, join with ss to form a ring.

Rnd 1: Ch2, 2hdc in ring, *ch2, 3hdc in ring; rep from * twice, ch2, ss in top of first 2-ch to join.

Join new color in any 2-ch corner sp.

Rnd 2: Ch2, 2hdc in corner sp, ch2, 3hdc in same corner sp, *ch1, 3hdc in next corner sp, ch2, 3hdc in same corner sp; rep from * twice, ch1, ss in top of first 2-ch to join.

With new color, join 4 squares using sc.

Using same color, work *1sc in each st to corner, [1sc, ch1, 1sc] in corner sp; rep from * around blanket, ss in first sc.

Fasten off, weave in ends.

FINISHING

Press blankets gently.

Fifi and the Stripey Ball

Fifi's stripey ball is almost as big as she is... she loves to chase after it and try to bite it, but it's too big for her mouth. But soon Fifi will grow and the ball won't, so she will succeed!

PUPPY

HEAD

Using A and 1.0mm (size 12) hook, make 6sc in magic circle, pull tail to close.
Rnd 1: 2sc in each sc. (12 sts)
Rnd 2: *1sc in next sc, 2sc in next sc; rep from * to end. (18 sts)
Rnd 3: *1sc in each of next 2 sc, 2sc in next sc; rep from * to end. (24 sts)
Rnds 4–8: 1sc in each sc. (24 sts)
Rnd 9: *1sc in each of next 2 sc, sc2tog; rep from * to end. (18 sts)
Rnd 10: *1sc in next sc, sc2tog; rep from * to end. (12 sts)
   Stuff firmly.
Rnd 11: Sc2tog around. (6 sts)
   Fasten off, leaving a long tail.

MUZZLE

Using A and 1.0mm (size 12) hook, make 12sc in magic circle, pull tail to close.
Rnds 1–2: 1sc in each sc. (12 sts)
   Fasten off, leaving a long tail.

EARS (MAKE 2)

Using A and 1.0mm (size 12) hook, and starting with a long tail, ch4.
Row 1: Skip 1 ch, 1sc in each of next 3 chs, turn. (3 sts)
Row 2: Ch1, 1sc in each sc, turn. (3 sts)
Row 3: Ch1, 1sc in first sc, 1hdc in next sc, [1sc, ss] in last sc.
   Fasten off.

SIZES
Puppy: 1⅜ in. long, 1 in. high
Ball: 1 in. diameter

ABBREVIATIONS
ch(s): chain, chains
hdc: half double crochet
rep: repeat
Rnd(s): round, rounds
sc: single crochet
sc2tog: single crochet 2 together decrease. Insert hook in next st, yo, pull through a loop. Without finishing st, insert hook in next st, yo and pull through a loop. Yo and pull through all three loops on hook
ss: slip stitch
st(s): stitch, stitches
yo: yarn over hook

MATERIALS
Puppy
- Small amount of laceweight yarn, such Rowan Kidsilk Haze 70% mohair/30% silk in pink (A)
- 1.0mm (size 12) steel crochet hook
- Toy stuffing
- Oddment of 6-strand embroidery floss in black and pink
- Sewing needle
- 4 in. narrow pink ribbon

Ball
- Oddments of No.5 crochet cotton, such as DMC Petra No.5 100% cotton, in desired colors (B)
- 1.5mm (size 8) steel crochet hook
- Toy stuffing
- Sewing needle

> Woof, woof!
> I'm going to get that ball this time!

BODY

Using A and 1.0mm (size 12) hook, make 6sc in magic circle, pull tail to close.

Rnd 1: 2sc in each sc. (12 sts)

Rnd 2: *1sc in next sc, 2sc in next sc; rep from * to end. (18 sts)

Rnd 3: *1sc in each of next 2 sc, 2sc in next sc; rep from * to end. (24 sts)

Rnds 4–13: 1sc in each sc. (24 sts)

Rnd 14: *1sc in each of next 2 sc, sc2tog; rep from * to end. (18 sts)

Rnd 15: *1sc in next sc, sc2tog; rep from * to end. (12 sts)

Stuff firmly.

Rnd 11: Sc2tog around. (6 sts)

Do not fasten off. To make tail, with yarn still attached to body, ch10, skip 1 ch, 1sc in each ch.

Fasten off.

LEGS (MAKE 4)

Using A and 1.0mm (size 12) hook, make 4sc in magic circle, pull tail to close.

Rnds 1–5: 1sc in each sc. (4 sts)

Fasten off, leaving a long tail.

FINISHING

Use yarn end to close hole in head, then sew head on body. Sew ears to head. Sew legs to body.

Embroider nose on muzzle in black embroidery floss then sew muzzle to front of head. Embroider eyes on head using black floss.

Wrap pink ribbon around neck for collar and use pink embroidery floss to work a round of running stitch along center of ribbon.

STRIPEY BALL

Change color every 2 rnds throughout.

Using 1.5mm (size 8) hook, make 6sc in magic circle, pull tail to close.

Rnd 1: 2sc in each sc. (12 sts)

Rnd 2: *1sc in next sc, 2sc in next sc; rep from * to end. (18 sts)

Rnd 3: *1sc in each of next 2 sc, 2sc in next sc; rep from * to end. (24 sts)

Rnds 4–7: 1sc in each sc. (24 sts)

Rnd 8: *1sc in each of next 2 sc, sc2tog; rep from * to end. (18 sts)

Rnd 9: *1sc in next sc, sc2tog; rep from * to end. (12 sts)

Stuff firmly.

Rnd 10: Sc2tog around. (6 sts)

Fasten off, leaving a long tail.

FINISHING

Use yarn end to close hole in ball.

Gus the Wiener Dog

Gus the dachshund is a happy fellow; he loves to chase lizards and snooze in the sunshine on the farm where he lives, and he loves chewing on his pink bone. Self-striping sock yarn means making Gus colorful is easy.

DACHSHUND

HEAD

Using A and 2.0mm (size 4) hook, make 6sc in magic circle, pull tail to close.

Rnd 1: 2sc in each sc. (12 sts)

Rnd 2: *1sc in next sc, 2sc in next sc; rep from * to end. (18 sts)

Rnds 3–6: 1sc in each sc. (18 sts)

Rnd 7: *1sc in next sc, sc2tog; rep from * to end. (12 sts)

    Insert safety eyes and secure. Stuff firmly.

Rnd 8: Sc2tog around. (6 sts)

    Fasten off, leaving a long tail. Leave bottom open.

MUZZLE

Using A and 2.0mm (size 4) hook, make 4sc in magic circle, pull tail to close.

Rnd 1: 1sc in each sc. (4 sts)

Rnd 2: *1sc in next sc, 2sc in next sc; rep from * once more. (6 sts)

Rnd 3: 1sc in each sc. (6 sts)

    Fasten off, leaving a long tail.

EARS (MAKE 2)

Using A and 2.0mm (size 4) hook, and starting with a long tail, ch4.

Row 1: Skip 1 ch, 1sc in each of next 3 chs, turn. (3 sts)

Row 2: Ch1, 1sc in each sc, turn.

Row 3: Ch1, 1sc in first sc, 1hdc in next sc, [1sc, ss] in last sc.

    Fasten off.

SIZES

Dachshund: 3 in. from nose to tip of tail, 1½ in. high

Bone: 1 in. long, ⅜ in. wide

Striped blanket: 2¼ x 2¼ in.

ABBREVIATIONS

beg: beginning

cont: continue

ch(s): chain, chains

hdc: half double crochet

rep: repeat

Rnd(s): round, rounds

sc: single crochet

sc2tog: single crochet 2 together decrease. Insert hook in next st, yo, pull through a loop. Without finishing st, insert hook in next st, yo and pull through a loop. Yo and pull through all three loops on hook

ss: slip stitch

st(s): stitch, stitches

yo: yarn over hook

MATERIALS

Dachshund

- Small amount of self-striping 4-ply sock wool, such as Rico Superba Mexico 75% Wool/25% Polyamide (A)
- 2.0mm (size 4) steel crochet hook
- Toy stuffing
- 1 x pair ¼ in. (6mm) safety eyes
- Black embroidery floss
- Sewing needle

Bone

- Small amount of No.8 crochet cotton, such as Rubi Perle No.8 100% cotton, in pink (B)
- 1.0mm (size 12) steel crochet hook
- Sewing needle

Striped blanket

- Small amount of 4-ply wool, such as Patons Fairytale Dreamtime 4-ply wool, in purple, blue and cream
- 2.0mm (size 4) steel crochet hook

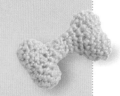

This is my bone— hands off!

BODY

Using A and 2.0mm (size 4) hook, make 6sc in magic circle, pull tail to close.

Rnd 1: 2sc in each sc. (12 sts)

Rnds 2–13: 1sc in each sc. (12 sts)

Stuff firmly.

Rnd 14: Sc2tog around. (6 sts)

Fasten off, leaving a long tail.

LEGS (MAKE 4)

Using A and 2.0mm (size 4) hook, make 6sc in magic circle, pull tail to close.

Rnds 1–3: 1sc in each sc. (6 sts)

Fasten off, leaving a long tail.

TAIL

Using A and 2.0mm (size 4) hook, make 4sc in magic circle, pull tail to close.

Rnds 1–3: 1sc in each sc. (4 sts)

Fasten off, leaving a long tail.

FINISHING

Embroider nose on muzzle using black embroidery floss, then sew muzzle to head. Sew ears to head.

Sew rem hole in body closed. Sew head, legs and tail to body.

BONE (MAKE 2 HALVES)

Using B and 1.0mm (size 12) hook, make 6sc in magic circle, pull tail to close.

Rnd 1: 2sc in each sc. (12 sts)

Ss in next st, fasten off.

Work a second piece as first to end of Round 1. Holding first circle next to new circle, begin working 1sc in each sc of first circle around, and then all the way around new circle, so they are joined. 1sc in each sc all the way around both circles again. (24 sts)

Sc2tog all the way around both circles.

Next rnd: [1sc in next sc, sc2tog] 4 times. (8 sts)

Work 3 rounds in sc.

Fasten off leaving a long tail.

Stuff bone end.

FINISHING

Sew both halves of bone together.

STRIPED BLANKET

Change color every 2 rows throughout.

Using 2.0mm (size 4) hook, ch 21.

Row 1: Skip first ch, 1sc in each ch to end, turn. (20 sts)

Row 2: Ch1, 1sc in each sc to end, turn. (20 sts)

Rows 3–20: As Row 2.

Fasten off.

FINISHING

Weave in ends. Press gently.

Harry the Cat Goes Fishing

Here, kitty, kitty! Harry the cat can always be tempted by a delicious fish, which is why you have to keep him away from the aquarium. Harry also enjoys playing with a bit of string or a feather on a stick. But his favorite thing is curling up on the lap of a warm human.

SIZES
Cat: 1¾ in. tall
Fish: 1¼ in. long

ABBREVIATIONS
hdc: half double crochet
rep: repeat
Rnd(s): round, rounds
sc: single crochet
sc2tog: single crochet 2 together decrease. Insert hook in next st, yo, pull through a loop. Without finishing st, insert hook in next st, yo and pull through a loop. Yo and pull through all three loops on hook
ss: slip stitch
st(s): stitch, stitches
yo: yarn over hook

MATERIALS
- Small amounts of No.5 crochet cotton, such as DMC Petra No.5 100% cotton, in blue (A), white (B) and peach (C)
- 1.5mm (size 8) steel crochet hook
- Toy stuffing
- Oddments of 6-strand cotton embroidery floss, in black and green
- Sewing needle
- Small piece of pink felt
- Craft/fabric adhesive

CAT
BODY AND HEAD
Using A, make 6sc in magic circle, pull tail to close.
Rnd 1: 2sc in each sc. (12 sts)
Rnd 2: *1sc in next sc, 2sc in next sc; rep from * to end. (18 sts)
Rnd 3: *1sc in each of next 2 sc, 2sc in next sc; rep from * to end. (24 sts)
Rnds 4–8: 1sc in each sc. (24 sts)
Rnd 9: Sc2tog around. (12 sts)
  Stuff firmly.
Rnds 10–13: 1sc in each sc. (12 sts)
Rnd 14: Sc2tog around. (6 sts)
  Fasten off, leaving a long tail.

EARS (MAKE 2)
Using A, ch3.
Row 1: Skip first ch, 1sc in next 2 chs, turn.
Row 2: Ch1, sc2tog.
  Fasten off, leaving a long tail.

TAIL
Using A, ch4.
Row 1: Skip first ch, 1sc in next 3 chs, turn.
Row 2: Ch1, 1sc in each of 3 sc, turn.
  Change to B, alternate colors every two rows.
Rows 3–10: Ch1, sc in each sc, turn.
Row 11: Ch2, 1hdc in each sc, ss in top of ch-2.
  Fasten off, leaving a long tail.

FISH
BODY (MAKE 2 HALVES)
Using C, ch2.
Row 1: Skip first ch, 1sc in next ch, turn.
Row 2: Ch1, 2sc in sc, turn.
Row 3: Ch1, 2sc in each sc to end, turn.
Rows 4–5: Ch1, 1sc in each sc to end, turn.
Row 6: Ch1, [sc2tog] twice, turn.
Row 7: Ch1, sc2tog.
  Fasten off.

FISH FINS (MAKE 2)
Using C, make 6sc in magic circle. Pull tail to make half-moon shape.

TAIL

Using C, [Ch4, skip 1 ch, 1sc in next 2 chs, ss in last] twice.

Fasten off, leaving a long tail.

FINISHING

Use yarn end to close hole in cat head. Sew ears to head and tail to body, curving it around.

Cut two small felt triangles and stick to front of ears. Cut a smaller felt triangle and stick to center of face for nose. Embroider French knots for eyes in green floss and stitch whiskers in black floss.

Sew two halves of fish together. Sew tail to one end of body and flat side of fins to sides of body.

Where's that cat? He won't catch me!

Catnip Mouse

This tiny mouse would be perfect as a gift for a new cat! Fill with a wee sachet of catnip or simply sprinkle some on after finishing—cats will find it completely irresistible.

Time to watch The Mouseketeers.

BODY

Make 6sc in magic circle, pull tail to close.

Rnd 1: *1sc in next sc, 2sc in next sc; rep from * to end. (9 sts)

Rnd 2: *1sc in each of next 2 sc, 2sc in next sc; rep from * to end. (12 sts)

Rnd 3: *1sc in each of next 2 sc, 2sc in next sc; rep from * to end. (16 sts)

Rnd 4: *1sc in each of next 3 sc, 2sc in next sc; rep from * to end. (20 sts)

Rnds 5–7: 1sc in each sc. (20 sts)

Rnd 8: *1sc in each of next 2 sc, sc2tog; rep from * to end. (15 sts)

Rnd 9: *1sc in next sc, sc2tog; rep from * to end. (10 sts)

Stuff firmly, inserting catnip along with toy stuffing if desired.

Rnd 10: Sc2tog around. (5 sts)

Insert hook in other side of rem hole and ss to close. Do not cut yarn.

Make tail: Ch10, fasten off.

EARS (MAKE 2)

Make 6sc in magic circle. Pull tail to make half-circle shape.

Row 1: Turn work, ch1, 1sc in each sc across, ss in 1-ch to close.

Fasten off, leaving long tail for sewing.

FINISHING

Weave in ends. Cut three short lengths of yarn and insert through snout to make whiskers—these will need to be tied firmly or omitted if the toy is being given to a cat.

Sew on ears. Sew French knots for eyes using black embroidery floss.

SIZE
1 in. long

ABBREVIATIONS
ch: chain
rem: remaining
rep: repeat
Rnd(s): round, rounds
sc: single crochet
sc2tog: single crochet 2 together decrease. Insert hook in next st, yo, pull through a loop. Without finishing st, insert hook in next st, yo and pull through a loop. Yo and pull through all three loops on hook
st(s): stitch, stitches
yo: yarn over hook

MATERIALS
- ¼ x ball, approx 11 yds, of No.8 crochet cotton, such as Rubi Perle No.8 100% cotton, in peach
- 1.4mm (size 9) steel crochet hook
- Toy stuffing
- Small sachet catnip (optional)
- Sewing needle
- Oddment of 6-strand cotton embroidery floss in black

Note: The mouse is made in continuous spiral rounds, so you will not join with a slip stitch. Use a stitch marker throughout to mark the first stitch of each round.

Mama and Baby Bunny

Mama is teaching Baby how to hop. Sometimes Baby has trouble because his feet are so big... but he's learning, and soon he and Mama will be hopping all over the place together!

MAMA BUNNY

HEAD/BODY

Using A, make 6sc in magic circle, pull tail to close.

Rnd 1: 2sc in each sc. (12 sts)

Rnd 2: *1sc in next sc, 2sc in next sc; rep from * to end. (18 sts)

Rnd 3: *1sc in each of next 2 sc, 2sc in next sc; rep from * to end. (24 sts)

Rnds 4–10: 1sc in each sc.

Rnd 11: *1sc in each of next 2 sc, sc2tog; rep from * to end. (18 sts)

Rnd 12: *1sc in next sc, sc2tog; rep from * to end. (12 sts)

Insert safety eyes and secure. Embroider X for nose in bright pink floss. Stuff firmly.

Rnd 13: Sc2tog around. (6 sts)

Fasten off, leaving a long tail.

ARMS (MAKE 2)

Using A, make 6sc in magic circle, pull tail to close.

Rnd 1: *1sc in next sc, 2sc in next sc; rep from * to end. (9 sts)

Rnds 2–3: 1sc in each sc.

Fasten off, leaving a long tail.

FOOT HALF (MAKE 2 EACH IN A AND B)

Ch5, skip 1 ch, 1sc in each of next 4 chs, turn. (4 sts)

Rows 1–4: Ch1, 1sc in each sc, turn.

Row 5: Ch2, hdc4tog.

Fasten off, leaving a long tail.

OUTER EAR (MAKE 2)

Using A, ch6, skip 1 ch, 1sc in each of next 5 chs, turn. (5 sts)

Rows 1–4: Ch1, 1sc in each sc, turn.

Row 5: Ch2, hdc2tog, 1hdc in next st, hdc2tog, turn. (3 sts)

Row 6: Ch1, sc3tog.

Fasten off, leaving a long tail.

INNER EAR

Using B, ch3, skip 1 ch, 1sc in each of next 2 chs, turn. (2 sts)

Rows 1–4: Ch1, 1sc in each sc, turn.

Row 5: Ch2, hdc2tog.

Fasten off, leaving a long tail.

SIZES

Mama bunny: 2⅛ in. tall

Baby bunny: 1¾ in. tall

Carrot: 1 in. long plus ⅜ in. for tops

ABBREVIATIONS

ch(s): chain, chains

hdc: half double crochet

hdc2tog: half double 2 together decrease. *Yo, insert hook into first st, yo, pull through a loop. Without finishing st, rep from * into next st. Yo and pull through all five loops on hook

hdc3tog: half double 3 together decrease. *Yo, insert hook into first st, yo, pull through a loop. Without finishing st, rep from * into each of next 2 sts. Yo and pull through all seven loops on hook

hdc4tog: half double 4 together decrease. *Yo, insert hook into first st, yo, pull through a loop. Without finishing st, rep from * into each of next 3 sts. Yo and pull through all nine loops on hook

sc: single crochet

sc2tog: single crochet 2 together decrease. Insert hook in next st, yo, pull through a loop. Without finishing st, insert hook in next st, yo and pull through a loop. Yo and pull through all three loops on hook

sc3tog: single crochet 3 together decrease. *Insert hook into first st, yo, pull through a loop. Without finishing st, rep from * into each of next 2 sts. Yo and pull yarn through all four loops on hook

rep: repeat

Rnd(s): round, rounds

st(s): stitch, stitches

yo: yarn over hook

MATERIALS

Bunnies

- ½ x 50g ball, approx 60m, of 4-ply baby yarn, such as Debbie Bliss Baby Cashmerino, in white (A)
- Small amount of 4-ply wool, such as Patons Fairytale Dreamtime 4-ply wool, in pink (B)
- 2.0mm (size 4) steel crochet hook
- 2 x pairs of safety eyes
- Toy stuffing
- Oddment of 6-strand embroidery floss in pink
- Sewing needle

Carrots

- 1 skein of 6-strand cotton embroidery floss in orange (A)
- Small amount of 6-strand cotton embroidery floss in green (B)
- 1.5mm (size 8) steel crochet hook

BABY BUNNY

HEAD/BODY

Using A, make 6sc in magic circle, pull tail to close.

Rnd 1: 2sc in each sc. (12 sts)

Rnds 2-7: 1sc in each sc. (12 sts)

Insert safety eyes and secure. Embroider X for nose in bright pink floss. Stuff firmly.

Rnd 8: Sc2tog around. (6 sts)

Fasten off, leaving a long tail.

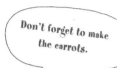

ARMS (MAKE 2)

Using A, make 6sc in magic circle, pull tail to close.

Rnds 1-2: 1sc in each sc. (6 sts)

Fasten off, leaving a long tail.

FOOT HALF (MAKE 2 EACH IN A AND B)

Ch3, skip 1 ch, 1sc in each of next 2 chs, turn. (2 sts)

Rows 1-2: Ch1, 1sc in each sc, turn.

Row 3: Ch2, hdc2tog.

Fasten off, leaving a long tail.

OUTER EAR (MAKE 2)

Using A, ch4, skip 1 ch, 1sc in each of next 3 chs, turn. (3 sts)

Rows 1-3: Ch1, 1sc in each sc, turn.

Row 4: Ch2, hdc3tog.

Fasten off, leaving a long tail.

INNER EAR (MAKE 2)

Using B, ch2, skip 1 ch, 1sc in next ch, turn. (1 st)

Rows 1-4: Ch1, 1sc in sc, turn.

Fasten off, leaving a long tail.

FINISHING

Use yarn ends to close hole in each body and to sew arms to bodies.

Sew feet halves in A and B together using whip st and white yarn. Stuff firmly. Sew feet to bodies.

Sew outer ear to inner ear using whip st and white yarn. Stuff firmly. Sew ears to bodies.

CARROT (MAKE 4 OR MORE)

Using A, make 6sc in magic circle; pull tail to close.

Rnds 1-6: 1sc in each sc. (6 sts)

Rnd 7: *1sc in next sc, sc2tog; rep from * to end. (4 sts)

Fasten off.

FINISHING

Cut three x 2-in. lengths of B. Insert hook in top of carrot, fold lengths in half over hook and pull through part way to form loop, then pull all cut ends through loop.

SIZES
Sheep: 2⅓ in. long, 1⅛ in. tall
Grass patch: 4⅛ x 3⅛ in.

ABBREVIATIONS

cont: continue

lpsc: loop single crochet. Insert hook into st, pick up both lengths of yarn looped over tensioning finger (near and far piece), pull both lengths back through st, adjust size of loop, then finish st as usual.

lpsc2tog: loop single crochet 2 together. *Insert hook into first st, pick up both lengths of yarn looped over tension finger and pull both back through st. Without finishing st, rep from * into next st. Yo and pull through all loops on hook

rep: repeat

Rnd(s): round, rounds

sc: single crochet

sc2tog: single crochet 2 together decrease. Insert hook in next st, yo, pull through a loop. Without finishing st, insert hook in next st, yo and pull through a loop. Yo and pull through all three loops on hook

ss: slip stitch

st(s): stitch, stitches

yo: yarn over hook

MATERIALS

Sheep

- Small amounts of No.5 crochet cotton, such as DMC Petra No.5 100% cotton, and laceweight yarn, such Rowan Kidsilk Haze 70% mohair/30% silk, in white (A)
- Oddment of No.5 crochet cotton such as DMC Petra No.5 100% cotton, in black (B)
- 2.0mm (size 4) and 1.5mm (size 8) steel crochet hooks
- Toy stuffing
- Sewing needle
- Scrap of white cotton

Grass patch

- Oddment of No.5 crochet cotton, such as DMC Petra No.5 100% cotton, in green (C)
- 2.0mm (size 4) steel crochet hook

Fuzzy Sheep

It's spring, and the tastiest new growth of green grass has arrived, so Clyde and Nigel, the two black-faced sheep, are munching away all day long. Their coats are long as they haven't been shorn yet, so they are extra fuzzy.

SHEEP

BODY

Work with wrong side facing and loops on outer side of body.

Using A and 2.0mm (size 4) hook, make 6sc in magic circle. Pull tail to close.

Rnd 1: 2lpsc in each sc. (12 sts)

Rnd 2: *1lpsc in next lpsc, 2lpsc in next lpsc; rep from * to end. (18 sts)

Rnds 3–5: 1lpsc in each lpsc. (18 sts)

Rnd 6: *1lpsc in next lpsc, lpsc2tog; rep from * to end. (12 sts)
   Stuff firmly.

Rnds 7–8: lpsc2tog around.
   Fasten off, leaving a long tail for sewing.

HEAD

Using B and 1.5mm (size 8) hook, make 4sc in magic circle. Pull tail to close.

Rnd 1: 2sc in each sc. (8 sts)

Rnd 2: 1sc in each sc. (8 sts)

Rnd 3: 2sc in each sc. (16 sts)

Rnds 4–7: 1sc in each sc. (16 sts)

Rnd 8: *1sc in each of next 2 sc, sc2tog; rep from * to end. (12 sts)

Rnd 9: Sc2tog around. (6 sts)
   Fasten off, leaving a long tail for sewing.

EARS (MAKE 2)

Using B, make 4sc in magic circle. Pull tail to close.

Rnds 1–3: 1sc in each sc.
   Fasten off, leaving a long tail for sewing.

LEGS (MAKE 4)

Using B and 1.5mm (size 8) hook, make 8sc in magic circle. Pull tail to close.

Rnds 1–3: 1sc in each sc. (8 sts)
   Ss in next sc.
   Fasten off, leaving a long tail for sewing.

> Note: Use one strand of crochet cotton and of laceweight mohair/silk yarn held together throughout.

> The grass is always greener on the other side of the fence.

FINISHING

Use yarn ends to close holes in body and head. Sew head and legs to body.
Attach ears to head.

Using white cotton, embroider eyes on either side of head.

GRASS PATCH FOR SHEEP

    Using C and 2.0mm (size 4) hook, ch31.

Row 1: Skip first ch, 1sc in each ch across, turn. (30 sts)

Row 2: Ch1, 1psc in each sc across, turn.

Row 3: Ch1, 1sc in each st across, turn.

    Rep Rows 2 and 3 another 10 times, then work Row 2 again.

    Fasten off, weave in ends.

Two Little Piggies

In autumn, Tucker and Wilfred the pigs like to gorge themselves on apples so it's really lucky they live in an apple orchard! Their favorites are the small tart green apples, but they'll take any type they can find.

PIGGIE

HEAD/BODY

Using A, make 8sc in magic circle, pull tail and ss in first st to close.

Rnd 1: Ch1, 1sc in back loop of each sc, ss in first st to close. (8 sts)

Rnd 2: Ch1, *1sc in next sc, 2sc in next sc; rep from * to end, ss in first st to close. (12 sts)

Rnd 3: Rep rnd 2. (18 sts)

Rnds 4-9: Ch1, 1sc in each sc, ss in first st to close. (18 sts)

Rnd 10: Ch1, *1sc in next sc, sc2tog; rep from * to end, ss in first st to close. (12 sts)

Stuff firmly.

Rnd 11: Ch1, sc2tog around, ss in first st to close. (6 sts)

Fasten off, leaving a long tail.

FEET (MAKE 4)

Using A, make 6sc in magic circle, pull tail to close.

Rnd 1: 1sc in back loop of each sc. (6 sts)

Fasten off, leaving a long tail.

EARS (MAKE 2)

Using A, ch4.

Row 1: Skip 1ch, 1sc in each of next 3 chs, turn.

Row 2: 1sc in first st, skip 1 st, 1sc in last st, turn.

Row 3: Sc2tog.

Fasten off, leaving a long tail.

TAIL

Using A, ch5.

Row 1: Skip first ch, 4sc in each of next 4 chs.

Fasten off, leaving a long tail.

FINISHING

Use yarn ends to close hole in piggie body and to sew on feet, ears, and tail. Embroider face, using black for eyes and bright pink for nostrils.

APPLE

Using B, make 6sc in magic circle, pull tail to close.

Rnd 1: 2sc in each sc. (12 sts)

Rnds 2-4: 1sc in each sc. (12 sts)

SIZES

Piggie: 1½ in. long

Apple: about ⅞ in. diameter

ABBREVIATIONS

ch(s): chain, chains

rep: repeat

Rnd(s): round, rounds

sc: single crochet

sc2tog: single crochet 2 together decrease. Insert hook in next st, yo, pull through a loop. Without finishing st, insert hook in next st, yo and pull through a loop. Yo and pull through all three loops on hook

ss: slip stitch

st(s): stitch, stitches

yo: yarn over hook

MATERIALS

Piggies

- Small amount of No.5 crochet cotton, such as DMC Petra No.5 100% cotton, in pink (A)
- 1.5mm (size 8) steel crochet hook
- Toy stuffing
- Oddments of 6-strand cotton embroidery floss split into 3 strands, in black and bright pink
- Sewing needle

Apples

- Small amount of No.5 crochet cotton, such as DMC Petra No.5 100% cotton, in green (B)
- 1.5mm (size 8) steel crochet hook
- Toy stuffing
- Sewing needle

Stuff firmly.

Rnd 5: Sc2tog around. (6 sts)

Fasten off, leaving a long tail.

FINISHING

Use yarn end to close hole in apple, then draw tail through top and bottom of apple several times, pulling tight to form dimples. Allow tail to emerge from top of apple, tie knot at desired stem length, then cut yarn.

This little piggie went to market, this little piggie stayed home...

CHAPTER 3

Home sweet home

Mini cupcakes and baskets of carrots... all the projects in this chapter are related to the home in some way. A tiny bowl of brightly colored wrapped candies is always inviting and the pretty beaded flower pot will certainly brighten up a windowsill or bookshelf. You can even make yourself a plate of sushi!

That's a smart wrap! Look out for those chopsticks.

Sensational Sushi

A tiny maki roll and salmon nigiri sit prettily on their own Japanese-style mini plate. They look good enough to eat!

MAKI
ROLL ENDS (MAKE 2)
Using A, make 6sc in magic circle, pull tail to close.
Rnd 1: 2sc in each sc (12 sts), ss in next st.
Fasten off A, attach B.
Rnd 2: *1sc in next sc, 2sc in next sc; rep from * to end. (18 sts)
Rnd 3: *1sc in each of next 2 sc, 2sc in next sc; rep from * to end. (24 sts)
Rnd 4: *1sc in each of next 3 sc, 2sc in next sc; rep from * to end. (30 sts)
Ss in next st, fasten off.

ROLL WRAPPER
Using C, ch32.
Row 1: Skip 2 chs, 1hdc in each of next 30 chs, turn. (30 sts)
Row 2: Ch2, 1hdc round post of each hdc from row below, turn.
Row 3: Ch2, 1hdc in each hdc across, turn.
Rep Rows 2 and 3 twice more.
Fasten off.

SALMON NIGIRI
SALMON PIECE SIDE (MAKE 2)
Using A, ch11.
Row 1: Skip 1 ch, 1sc in each of next 10 chs, turn. (10 sts)
Rows 2–15: Ch1, 1sc in each sc across, turn.
Fasten off.

RICE
Using B, ch11.
Rnd 1: Skip 1 ch, 3sc in next ch, 1sc in each of next 8 chs, 3sc in last ch. Working down other side of chain, 1sc in each of next 8 chs. (22 sts)
Rnd 2: 2sc in each of next 3 sc, 1sc in each of next 8 sc, 2sc in each of next 3 sc, 1sc in each of next 8 sc. (28 sts)

SIZES
Sushi: maki roll 1¼ in. across, nigiri 2 in. long, 1 in. high
Plate: 3 in. long, 1½ in. wide

ABBREVIATIONS
ch(s): chain, chains
hdc: half double crochet
rep: repeat
Rnd(s): round, rounds
sc: single crochet
sc2tog: single crochet 2 together decrease. Insert hook in next st, yo, pull through a loop. Without finishing st, insert hook in next st, yo and pull through a loop. Yo and pull through all three loops on hook
ss: slip stitch
st(s): stitch, stitches
yo: yarn over hook

MATERIALS
- Small amounts of No.5 crochet cotton, such as DMC Petra No.5 100% cotton, in peach (A), white (B), black (C), and light blue (D)
- 1.5mm (size 8) steel crochet hook
- Toy stuffing
- Sewing needle

Rnd 3: [1sc in next sc, 2sc in next sc] 3 times, 1sc in each of next 8 sc, [1sc in next sc, 2sc in next sc] 3 times, 1sc in each of next 8 sc. (34 sts)

Rnd 4: [1sc in each of next 2 sc, 2sc in next sc] 3 times, 1sc in each of next 8 sc, [1sc in each of next 2 sc, 2sc in next sc] 3 times, 1sc in each of next 8 sc. (40 sts)

Rnd 5: [1sc in each of next 3 sc, 2sc in next sc] 3 times, 1sc in each of next 8 sc, [1sc in each of next 3 sc, 2sc in next sc] 3 times, 1sc in each of next 8 sc. (46 sts)

Rnds 6–8: 1sc in each sc. (46 sts)

Rnd 9: [1sc in each of next 3 sc, sc2tog] 3 times, 1sc in each of next 8 sc, [1sc in each of next 3 sc, sc2tog] 3 times, 1sc in each of next 8 sc. (40 sts)

Rnd 10: [1sc in each of next 2 sc, sc2tog] 3 times, 1sc in each of next 8 sc, [1sc in each of next 2 sc, sc2tog] 3 times, 1sc in each of next 8 sc. (34 sts)

Rnd 11: [1sc in next sc, sc2tog] 3 times, 1sc in each of next 8 sc, [1sc in next sc, sc2tog] 3 times, 1sc in each of next 8 sc. (28 sts)

Rnd 12: [Sc2tog] 3 times, 1sc in each of next 8 sc, [sc2tog] 3 times, 1sc in each of next 8 sc. (22 sts)

Stuff firmly.

Rnd 13: Sc2tog around, ss in next sc. (11 sts)

Fasten off, leaving a long tail.

NIGIRI WRAPPER

Using C, ch6.

Row 1: Skip 1 ch, 1sc in each of next 5 chs. (30 sts)

Rows 2–31: Ch1, 1sc in each sc across.

Fasten off, leaving a long tail.

FINISHING

With B, sew maki roll ends to wrapper with whip stitch, stuffing before closing second end.

Sew diagonal lines of back stitch in B on one side of salmon piece side. With A, join two sides with sc join, stuffing lightly before closing last side.

Use yarn end to sew hole in rice closed. Use yarn end to sew nigiri wrapper into a loop. Place around salmon piece and rice.

MINI PLATE

Using D, ch31.

Row 1: Skip 1 ch, 1sc in each of rem 30 chs, turn.

Rows 2–18: Ch1, 1sc in each sc across, turn.

Begin working in rounds for edging.

Rnds 1–2: Ch1, 1sc down sides and into each sc around whole plate, make 1ch at each corner.

Fasten off.

A Japanese-style plate is ideal to display your pieces of sushi.

Scrumptious Cake and Tart

Why not have a tea party with these yummy-looking goodies? Make the slice of cake in your favorite 'flavors' and the tart with the 'berries' you love the best.

Make the berries in any bright color...

CAKE SLICE

LAYERS
Using A, ch15.
Row 1: Skip first ch, 1sc in each ch to end, turn. (14 sts)
Rows 2–3: Ch1, 1sc in each sc to end, turn.
  Change to B.
Row 4: Ch1, 1sc in each sc to end, turn.
  Change to A.
Rows 5–7: Ch1, 1sc in each sc to end, turn.
  Fasten off.

TOP/BOTTOM (MAKE 2)
Using B and starting with a long tail, ch9.
Row 1: Skip first ch, 1sc in each ch to end, turn. (8 sts)
Row 2: Ch1, sc2tog, 1sc in each of next 4 sc, sc2tog, turn. (6 sts)
Row 3: Ch1, sc2tog, 1sc in each of next 2 sc, sc2tog, turn. (4 sts)
Row 4: Ch1, [sc2tog] twice, turn. (2 sts)
Row 5: Ch1, sc2tog.
  Fasten off, leaving a long tail.

BACK
Using B, ch9
Row 1: Skip 1ch, 1sc in each ch to end, turn. (8 sts)
Rows 2–7: Ch 1, sc in each sc to end, turn.
  Fasten off.

SIZES

Cake slice: 1¼ in. tall
Tart: 1⅜ in. diameter

ABBREVIATIONS

ch(s): chain, chains
hdc: half double crochet
rep: repeat
Rnd(s): round, rounds
sc: single crochet
sc2tog: single crochet 2 together decrease. Insert hook in next st, yo, pull through a loop. Without finishing st, insert hook in next st, yo and pull through a loop. Yo and pull through all three loops on hook
ss: slip stitch
st(s): stitch, stitches
yo: yarn over hook

MATERIALS

- Small amounts of No.5 crochet cotton, such as DMC Petra No.5 100% cotton, in yellow (A), pink (B), beige (C) and red (D)
- 1.5mm (size 8) steel crochet hook
- Sewing needle
- Toy stuffing
- Craft/fabric adhesive (optional)

FINISHING

Use yarn ends to attach top and bottom to layer piece of cake slice using sc. Attach back to cake slice using sc, stuffing before closing the last side.

To make frill at top back of slice, attach yarn in first st, ch2, 2hdc in same st, ss in next st, *3hdc in next st, ss in next st; rep from * to end.

Fasten off.

TART

TART BASE

Using C, make 6sc in magic circle, pull tail to close.

Rnd 1: 2sc in each sc. (12 sts)
Rnd 2: *1sc in next sc, 2sc in next sc; rep from * to end. (18 sts)
Rnd 3: *1sc in each of next 2 sc, 2sc in next sc; rep from * to end. (24 sts)
Rnd 4: *1sc in each of next 2 sc, 2sc in next sc; rep from * to end. (32 sts)
Rnd 5: 1sc in back loop of each sc. (32 sts)
Rnd 6: 1sc in each sc. (32 sts)
Rnd 7: Ch2, 4hdc in first st, skip 1 st, ss in next st, *skip 1 st, 5hdc in next st, skip 1 st, ss in next st; rep from * to end.

Fasten off.

BERRIES (MAKE 8)

Using D, make 6sc in magic circle, pull tail to close.

Rnds 1–2: 1sc in each sc. (6 sts)

Fasten off, leaving a long tail.

FINISHING

Stuff each berry firmly. Use yarn end to close hole. Berries can be placed loosely in tart or stitched/glued into place.

Mini Cupcakes on a Plate

These teeny cupcakes look just like the real thing. Arrange them on their plate for your next doll tea party or give as tiny favors at your own tea party.

Life is just a cake with cherries.

CUPCAKE

BASE

Using A, ch4, join with ss to form ring.

Rnd 1: Ch3, 11dc in ring; ss in top of ch-3 to join.

Rnd 2: Ch1, 1sc in back loop of each dc, join with ss in first sc.

Rnd 3: Ch3, 1dc around post of each sc from rnd below, join with ss in top of first ch-3.

Rnd 4: Ch2, 1dc around post of each dc from rnd below, join with ss in top of first ch-2.

    Fasten off.

TOP

Using B, make 6sc in magic circle, pull tail to close.

Rnd 1: 2sc in each sc. (12 sts)

Rnd 2: *1sc in each of next 2 sc, 2sc in next sc; rep from * to end. (16 sts)

Rnd 3: Working in front loops of previous rnd sts only, *5hdc in next st, skip 1 st, ss in next st, skip 1 st; rep from * to end, ss in last st to close.

    Fasten off, leaving a long tail.

PLATE

Using C, make 6sc in magic circle, pull tail to close.

Rnd 1: 2sc in each sc. (12 sts)

Rnd 2: *1sc in next sc, 2sc in next sc; rep from * to end of round. (18 sts)

Rnd 3: *1sc in each of next 2 sc, 2sc in next sc; rep from * to end. (24 sts)

Rnd 4: *1sc in each of next 3 sc, 2sc in next sc; rep from * to end. (30 sts)

Rnd 5: *1sc in each of next 4 sc, 2sc in next sc; rep from * to end. (36 sts)

Rnd 6: *1sc in each of next 5 sc, 2sc in next sc; rep from * to end. (42 sts)

Rnd 7: *1sc in each of next 6 sc, 2sc in next sc; rep from * to end. (48 sts)

Rnd 8: Ss in next st, *ch3, ss in next st; rep from * to end.

    Fasten off.

FINISHING

Using C, embroider cherry in center of cupcake top. Stuff cake base and then sew top to base with yarn end of top. Weave in ends.

SIZES

Cupcake: About ⅞ in. tall

Plate: 2 in. diameter

ABBREVIATIONS

ch(s): chain, chains

dc: double crochet

hdc: half double crochet

rep: repeat

Rnd(s): round, rounds

sc: single crochet

ss: slip stitch

st(s): stitch, stitches

MATERIALS

- Small amount of No.5 crochet cotton, such as DMC Petra No.5, in pale blue (A), pink (B) and red (C)
- 1.5mm (size 8) steel crochet hook
- Sewing needle
- Toy stuffing

Flower Box and Pot with Doilies

Sweet little flowers and sparkly beads adorn this tiny box and pot. Use to bring fresh life to a minuscule nook in your home, even in the depths of winter—and make the co-ordinating doilies to finish the look.

Green glass beads make the flowers sparkle in the sun.

BOX

SIDES/BOTTOM (MAKE 5)
Ch7.
Row 1: Skip 1 ch, 1sc in next 6 chs, turn. (6 sts)
Rows 2–6: 1sc in each sc across, turn.
　　Fasten off.

BASE FOR FLOWERS
Make 6sc in magic circle, pull tail to close.
Rnd 1: 2sc in each sc to end. (12 sts)
Rnd 2: *1sc in next sc, 2sc in next sc; rep from * to end. (18 sts)
Rnd 3: *1sc in each of next 2 sc, 2sc in next sc; rep from * to end. (24 sts)
Rnds 4–6: 1sc in each sc. (24 sts)
　　Fasten off.

POT

SIDES/BOTTOM
Make 6sc in magic circle, pull tail to close.
Rnd 1: 2sc in each sc to end. (12 sts)
Rnd 2: *1sc in next sc, 2sc in next sc; rep from * to end. (18 sts)
Rnd 3: 1sc in back loop of each sc. (18 sts)
Rnds 4–8: 1sc in each sc to end. (18 sts)

SIZES

Flower box: 1¼ in. tall, 1 in. across
Flower pot: 1¼ in. tall, ⅞ in. diameter
Round doily: 1⅛ in. diameter
Star doily: 2¼ in. from tip to tip

ABBREVIATIONS

ch(s): chain, chains
dc: double crochet
dc2tog: double 2 together decrease.
*Yo, insert hook into first st, yo, pull through a loop, yo and pull through first 2 loops on hook. Without finishing st, rep from * into next st. Yo, pull yarn through all three loops on hook
hdc: half double crochet
hdc2tog: half double 2 together decrease. *Yo, insert hook into first st, yo, pull through a loop. Without finishing st, rep from * into next st. Yo, pull yarn through all five loops on hook
rep: repeat
sc: single crochet
sp: space
ss: slip stitch
st(s): stitch, stitches
yo: yarn over hook

MATERIALS

Box, pot, and flower bases
- Small amount of No.5 crochet cotton, such as DMC Petra No.5 100% cotton, in desired colors
- 1.5mm (size 8) steel crochet hook
- Toy stuffing, if desired
- Sewing needle

Flowers
- Small amount of No.8 crochet cotton, such as Rubi Perle No.8 100% cotton, in desired colors
- 1.4mm (size 9) steel crochet hook
- Glass beads
- Embroidery floss or sewing thread
- Sewing needle

Doilies
- Small amount of No.8 crochet cotton, such as Rubi Perle No.8 100% cotton, in desired color
- 1.5mm (size 8) steel crochet hook

Rnd 9: With contrasting color if desired, ch3, 1dc round post of each sc in round below.

Fasten off.

BASE FOR FLOWERS

Make 6sc in magic circle, pull tail to close.

Rnd 1: 2sc in each sc. (12 sts)

Rnds 2–4: 1sc in each sc. (12 sts)

Fasten off.

FLOWERS (MAKE AS MANY AS DESIRED)

Ch4, join with ss to first ch to form a ring.

Rnd 1: Ch1, make 8sc into circle, join with ss to first sc. (8 sts)

Rnd 2: *Ch2, 1hdc in same st, 1hdc in next st, ch2, ss in same st, ss in next st; rep from * to end. (4 petals made)

Fasten off, leaving a long tail.

FINISHING

Join four side pieces and one bottom piece into box shape using sc.

Use yarn end to sew flowers to flower bases. Use one strand of embroidery floss or machine sewing thread to attach a bead to center of each flower. Place flower base into box or pot; toy stuffing can be used to fill out each piece if desired.

ROUND DOILY

Ch4, join with ss to first ch to form a ring.

Rnd 1: Ch1, [ch3, 1sc in circle] 5 times, ch3, ss in first ch to join.

Rnd 2: Ch1, 1sc in first ch-3 sp, *ch3, 1sc in next ch-3 sp; rep from * to end, replacing last sc with ss into first sc.

Rnd 3: Ss in next ch-3 sp, ch2, 4hdc in same sp, *ch1, 5hdc in next ch-3 sp; rep from * to end, ch1, ss in top of first ch-2.

Rnd 4: Ch2, 1hdc in next 2 hdc, hdc2tog, ch3, skip ch-1 sp, *hdc2tog, 1hdc in next st, hdc2tog, ch3, skip ch-1 sp; rep from * to end, ss in top of first hdc.

Rnd 5: Ch2, hdc2tog, ch3, 1dc in ch3-sp, ch3, *1hdc in next hdc, hdc2tog, ch3, 1dc in ch-3 sp, ch3; rep from * to end, ss in top of first ch-2.

Fasten off.

Notes: To make a striped box as shown, change color every 2 rows. The flower box shown here has six flowers; there are four in the flower pot.

STAR DOILY

Ch4, join with ss to first ch to form a ring.

Rnd 1: Ch5, [1dc in ring, ch2] 5 times, join with ss in third ch of first ch-5.

Rnd 2: Ss in first ch-2 sp, ch3, 4dc in same sp, ch1, *5dc in next ch-2 sp, ch1; rep from * to end, ss in top of first ch-3.

Note: Rows 3–5 will be worked back and forth in rows on one star point at a time. Cut yarn and rejoin in the next dc group of Round 2 each time, then repeat Rows 3–5 for each point.

Row 3: Ch2, 1dc in next 2 sts, dc2tog, turn.

Row 4: Ch3, dc2tog, turn.

Row 5: Ch2, 1hdc in next st.

Fasten off.

Wee Carrots in a Basket

Is there anything nicer than fresh, crunchy carrots picked from your own garden? Make this lovely basket heaped high with carrots for a dolls' house garden, or as a gift for your favorite gardener.

Notes: When using the embroidery floss, use all six strands throughout. One skein of embroidery floss will make about six carrots.

CARROT

ROOT (MAKE 4 OR MORE)

Using A, make 6sc in magic circle; pull tail to close.

Rnds 1–6: 1sc in each sc. (6 sts)

Rnd 7: *1sc in next sc, sc2tog; rep from * to end. (4 sts)

Fasten off.

TOP (MAKE ONE FOR EACH ROOT)

Cut three x 2-in. lengths of B. Insert hook in top of carrot, fold lengths in half over hook and pull through part way to form loop, then pull cut ends through loop.

BASKET

BASE/SIDES

Using C, ch8.

Rnd 1: Skip 1 ch, 1sc in each of next 6 chs, 3sc in last ch. Working down opposite side of ch, 1sc in each of next 5 chs, 2sc in last ch. (16 sts)

Rnd 2: 2sc in next st, 1sc in each of next 5 sts, 2sc in each of next 3 sts, 1sc in each of next 5 sts, 2sc in each of next 2 sts. (22 sts)

Rnd 3: 2sc in next st, 1sc in each of next 7 sts, 2sc in each of next 4 sts, 1sc in each of next 7 sts, 2sc in each of next 3 sts. (30 sts)

Rnd 4: 2sc in next st, 1sc in each of next 10 sts, [2sc in next st, 1sc in next st] twice, 2sc in next st, 1sc in next 10 sts, [2sc in next st, 1sc in next st] twice. (36 sts)

Rnd 5: 1sc in back loop of each st. (36 sts)

Rnds 6–9: 1sc in each sc. (36 sts)

Rnd 10: Ss in next st, *ch3, skip 1 st, ss in next st; rep from * to end.
   Fasten off.

HANDLE

Using C, ch16.

Row 1: Skip 1 ch, 1sc in each sc, turn. (15 sts)

Row 2: *Ch3, skip 1 st, ss in next st; rep from * to end. Working down opposite side of ch, rep Row 2.
   Fasten off.

FINISHING

Sew handle to inner rim of basket.

SIZES

Carrot: 1 in. long plus ⅜ in. for tops
Basket: 1¼ in. high, 1 in. wide

ABBREVIATIONS

ch(s): chain, chains
rep: repeat
Rnd(s): round, rounds
sc: single crochet
sc2tog: single crochet 2 together decrease. Insert hook in next st, yo, pull through a loop. Without finishing st, insert hook in next st, yo and pull through a loop. Yo and pull through all three loops on hook
ss: slip stitch
st(s): stitch, stitches
yo: yarn over hook

MATERIALS

Carrots

• 1 skein of 6-strand cotton embroidery floss in orange (A)
• Small amount of 6-strand cotton embroidery floss in green (B)
• 1.5mm (size 8) steel crochet hook

Basket

• Small amount of No.5 crochet cotton, such as Anchor Artiste No.5, in beige (C)
• 1.5mm (size 8) steel crochet hook
• Sewing needle

Don't forget to make a basket to carry the carrots...

Fresh Fruit Bowl

This is the teeniest tiniest fruit bowl imaginable—it's perfect for a dolls' house or for displaying amongst other small treasures. This project does require some patience, but the result is worth it.

Notes:
The orange and apple are made with continuous spiral rounds, so do not join with slip stitch. The banana and bowl are made with joined rounds; slip stitches and chains are noted in the pattern. Use a stitch marker to mark the first stitch of each round.

FRUIT

ORANGE

Using A and 1.5mm (size 8) hook, make 6sc in magic circle. Pull tail to close.

Rnd 1: 2sc in each sc. (12 sts)

Rnd 2: *1sc in next sc, 2sc in next sc; rep from * to end. (18 sts)

Rnds 3–5: 1sc in each sc. (18 sts)

Rnd 6: *1sc in next sc, sc2tog; rep from * to end. (12 sts)

   Stuff firmly.

Rnd 7: Sc2tog around. (6 sts)

   Cut yarn, leaving a long tail. Thread through rem sts and pull tight to close.

ORANGE LEAF

Using B and 1.5mm (size 8) hook, ch5, skip first st, 1sc in next st, 1hdc in next st, 2dc in next st, ss in last st.

   Cut yarn, leaving a long tail for sewing.

APPLE

Using C and 1.5mm (size 8) hook, make 8sc in magic circle. Pull tail to close.

Rnd 1: 2sc in each sc. (16 sts)

Display the pieces of fruit in a pretty striped fruit bowl.

SIZES

Apple/Orange: about ½ in. diameter
Banana: 1 in. long
Bowl: 1¼ in. diameter

ABBREVIATIONS

ch: chain
dc: double crochet
hdc: half double crochet
rem: remaining
rep: repeat
Rnd(s): round, rounds
sc: single crochet
sc2tog: single crochet 2 together decrease. Insert hook in next st, yo, pull through a loop. Without finishing st, insert hook in next st, yo and pull through a loop. Yo and pull through all three loops on hook
ss: slip stitch
st(s): stitch, stitches
yo: yarn over hook

MATERIALS

Orange
- Oddments of 6-strand cotton embroidery floss in orange (A)
- Oddment of 6-strand cotton embroidery floss in dark green (B)
- 1.5mm (size 8) steel crochet hook
- Toy stuffing
- Sewing needle

Apple and banana
- Oddments of No.8 crochet cotton, such as Rubi Perle No.8 100% cotton, in pale green (C) and yellow (D)
- Oddment of 6-strand cotton embroidery floss in dark green (B)
- 1.5mm (size 8) steel crochet hook
- Toy stuffing
- Sewing needle

Fruit bowl
- Oddments of No.8 crochet cotton, such as Rubi Perle No.8 100% cotton, in two colors
- 1.75mm (size 6) steel crochet hook

Rnds 2–5: 1sc in each sc. (16 sts)

Rnd 6: *1sc in each of next 2 sc, sc2tog; rep from * to end. (12 sts)

Rnd 7: *1sc in next sc, sc2tog; rep from * to end. (8 sts)

Stuff firmly.

Rnd 8: Sc2tog around. (4 sts)

Cut yarn, leaving a long tail. Thread through rem sts and pull tight to close.

BANANA

Using C and 1.5mm (size 8) hook, make 4sc in magic circle, pull tail to close and join with ss in first sc.

Rnds 1–2: Ch1, 1sc in each sc, join with ss in first sc. (4 sc)

Change to D.

Rnd 3: Ch1, *1sc in next sc, 2sc in next sc; rep from * once, join with ss in first sc. (6 sts)

Rnd 4: Ch1, 1sc in each sc, join with ss in first sc. (6 sts)

Rnd 5: Ch1, *1sc in next sc, 2sc in next sc; rep from * twice, join with ss in first sc. (9 sts)

Rnd 6: Ch1, 1sc in each sc, join with ss in first sc. (9 sts)

Rnd 7: Ch1, *1sc in next sc, sc2tog; rep from * twice, join with ss in first sc. (6 sts)

Rnd 8: Ch1, 1sc in each sc, join with ss in first sc. (6 sts)

Rnd 9: Ch1, *1sc in next sc, sc2tog; rep from * once, join with ss in first sc. (4 sts)

Cut yarn, leaving a long tail. Thread through rem sts and pull tight to close.

FINISHING

Sew leaf to top of orange.

For apple, pass length of B through top and bottom of apple several times and pull tight to form dimples. Allow end of floss to emerge from top of apple, tie knot at top of desired length for stem and then trim ends.

FRUIT BOWL

Change color each round.

Using 1.75mm (size 6) hook, make 6sc in magic circle, pull tail to close and join with ss in first sc.

Rnd 1: Ch1, 2sc in each sc, join with ss in first sc. (12 sts)

Rnd 2: Ch1, *1sc in next sc, 2sc in next sc; rep from * to end, join with ss in first sc. (18 sts)

Rnd 3: Ch1, *1sc in each of next 2 sc, 2sc in next sc; rep from * to end, join with ss in first sc. (24 sts)

Rnd 4: Ch1, *1sc in each of next 3 sc, 2sc in next sc; rep from * to end, join with ss in first sc. (30 sts)

Rnd 5: Ch1, *1sc in each of next 4 sc, 2sc in next sc; rep from * to end, join with ss in first sc. (36 sts)

Rnd 6: Ch1, *1sc in each of next 5 sc, 2sc in next sc; rep from * to end, join with ss in first sc. (42 sts)

Rnds 7–9: Ch1, 1sc in each sc, join with ss in first sc. (42 sts)

Cut yarn, weave in ends.

Notes: When crocheting with embroidery floss be sure to use a firm tension and be careful not to split the strands with the hook. Use all 6 strands throughout.

Candies: 1½ in. long
Bowl: 3 in. diameter

ABBREVIATIONS

dc: double crochet
hdc: half double crochet
rep: repeat
Rnd(s): round, rounds
sc: single crochet
sc2tog: single crochet 2 together
decrease. Insert hook in next st, yo,
pull through a loop. Without finishing
st, insert hook in next st, yo and pull
through a loop. Yo and pull through
all three loops on hook
ss: slip stitch
st(s): stitch, stitches
yo: yarn over hook

MATERIALS

Candies

- Small amount of 4-ply wool, such
  as Patons Dreamtime 4-ply wool, in
  blue (A)
- Small amount of 4-ply wool, such
  as Patons Dreamtime 4-ply wool, in
  pink (B)
- 2.0mm (size 4) steel crochet hook
- Toy stuffing
- Sewing needle

Dish

- ¼ x 50g ball, approx 33 yds, of 4-ply
  baby yarn, such as Debbie Bliss
  Baby Cashmerino 4-ply, in cream (C)
- 2.0mm (size 4) steel crochet hook

Notes: Candy
wrapper ends are made
separately from main ball.
Main ball and candy dish are
worked in continuous spiral
rounds, so do not join with a slip
stitch. Use a stitch marker
throughout to mark first
stitch of each round.

Sweets for the Sweet

These adorable candies look good enough to eat
and they can be made in any color you desire, with
stripes or without. Pile several into the pretty
candy dish and display—you could also use the
small dish as an alternative to hold the fruit on
page 69–70, or to keep tiny items of value safe.

CANDIES

MAIN BALL

Using A or B, make 6sc into magic circle, pull tail to close.

Rnd 1: 2sc in each sc. (12 sts)

Rnd 2: *1sc in next sc, 2sc in next sc; rep from * to end. (18 sts)
   If making striped sweets, change color for Rounds 3 and 5.

Rnds 3–6: 1sc in each sc. (18 sts)

Rnd 7: *1sc in next sc, sc2tog; rep from * to end. (12 sts)
   Stuff firmly.

Rnd 8: Sc2tog around. (6 sts)
   Cut yarn, leaving a long tail. Weave through rem sts and pull tight
to close.

WRAPPER END (MAKE 2 FOR EACH CANDY)

Using a contrast color to the candy if desired and leaving a long tail for
sewing on, ch7, 2dc in fourth ch from hook, 1hdc in next ch, 1sc in next ch,
ss in next ch.
   Working down other side of ch, ss in next ch, 1sc in next ch, 1hdc in
next ch, 2dc in next ch, ch2, ss in same st as last dc.
   Cut yarn, weave in last end.

FINISHING

Sew wrapper end to each end of candies.

CANDY DISH

Using C, make 6sc into magic circle, pull tail to close.

Rnd 1: 2sc in each sc. (12 sts)

Rnd 2: *1sc in next sc, 2sc in next sc; rep from * around. (18 sts)

Rnd 3: *1sc in each of next 2 sc, 2sc in next sc; rep from * around. (24 sts)

Rnd 4: *1sc in each of next 3 sc, 2sc in next sc; rep from * around.
   (30 sts)

Rnd 5: *1sc in each of next 4 sc, 2sc in next sc; rep from *
   around. (36 sts)

Rnd 6: *1sc in each of next 5 sc, 2sc in next sc; rep from *
   around. (42 sts)

Rnd 7: *1sc in each of next 6 sc, 2sc in next sc; rep from * around. (48 sts)

Rnd 8: *1sc in each of next 7 sc, 2sc in next sc; rep from * around. (54 sts)

Rnds 9–13: 1sc in each sc. (54 sts)

Rnd 14: (Picot edging) *Ss in each of next 2 sc, ch3, ss in same sc as last ss; rep from * to end, ss in first st to end.

    Cut yarn.

FINISHING

Weave in ends. Pile candies into bowl.

You can never have too many candies.

CHAPTER 4

Pretty things

We love to adorn our home and ourselves with pretty things, so why not make some? Fashion a tiny bead or flower bracelet for a special person (or yourself!), create a lucky gift with the Four Leaf Clover Keychain, or decorate a treasured spot with the Russian Doll Sisters. There are also great ideas for the festive season, such as the Snowman and Bauble Cover, which can be displayed for maximum sweet effect with the Itty-bitty Snowflake Garland.

Russian Doll Sisters

Ekaterina, Elena, and Eva are three sisters who
live in the highest onion dome of a very ancient
building in St Petersburg, Russia. They like to eat
blini with fresh strawberries and embroider
themselves new dresses.

Hello Elena! Let's go on a picnic and eat some strawberries.

EVA

Using MC and 1.4mm (size 9) hook, make 6sc in magic circle.

Rnd 1: 2sc in each sc. (12 sts)

Rnd 2: *1sc in next sc, 2sc in next sc; rep from * to end. (18 sts)

Rnd 3: *1sc in each of next 2 sc, 2sc in next sc; rep from * to end. (24 sts)

Rnds 4–7: 1sc in each sc. (24 sts)

Rnd 8: 1sc in back loop of each sc. (24 sts)

    Change to CC.

Rnd 9: *1sc in each of next 3 sc, 2sc in next sc; rep from * to end. (30 sts)

Rnds 10–11: 1sc in each sc. (30 sts)

Rnd 12: *1sc in each of next 4 sc, 2sc in next sc; rep from * to end. (36 sts)

Rnds 13–14: 1sc in each sc. (36 sts)

Rnd 15: *1sc in each of next 4 sc, sc2tog; rep from * to end. (30 sts)

Rnd 16: *1sc in each of next 3 sc, sc2tog; rep from * to end. (24 sts)

SIZES

Eva: 1½ in. tall
Elena: 1¾ in. tall
Ekaterina: 2 in. tall

ABBREVIATIONS

beg: beginning
dc: double crochet
hdc: half double crochet
sc: single crochet
sc2tog: single crochet 2 together
decrease. Insert hook in next st,
yo, pull through a loop. Without
finishing st, insert hook in next st,
yo and pull through a loop. Yo and
pull through all three loops on hook
st(s): stitch, stitches
tr: treble crochet
rem: remaining
rep: repeat
Rnd(s): round, rounds
yo: yarn over hook

MATERIALS

Eva (smallest Russian doll)

- ¼ x ball, approx 11 yds, of No.8
  crochet cotton, such as Rubi Perle
  No.8 100% cotton, in peach (MC)
- ¼ x ball, approx 11 yds, of No.8
  crochet cotton, such as Rubi Perle
  No.8 100% cotton, in turquoise (CC)
- 1.4mm (size 9) steel crochet hook

Elena (middle Russian doll)

- ⅟₁₆ x ball, approx 27 yds, of No.5
  crochet cotton, such as DMC Petra
  Perle No.5 100% cotton, in pale
  blue (MC)
- ⅟₁₆ x ball, approx 27 yds, of No.5
  crochet cotton, such as DMC Petra
  Perle No.5 100% cotton, in lilac (CC)
- 1.75mm (size 6) steel crochet hook

Ekaterina (biggest Russian doll)

- ⅟₁₆ x ball, approx 37 yds, of 4-ply
  cotton yarn, such as Wendy
  Supreme 4-ply 100% cotton, in
  pink (MC)
- ⅟₁₆ x ball, approx 37 yds, of 4-ply
  cotton yarn, such as Wendy
  Supreme 4-ply 100% cotton, in
  green (CC)
- 2.0mm (size 4) steel crochet hook

All dolls

- Toy stuffing
- Sewing needle
- Cream felt for face and dress panel
- Yellow felt for hair
- Oddments of embroidery floss in
  green, pink, and blue
- Powder blush for cheeks
- Craft/fabric adhesive

Rnd 17: *1sc in each of next 2 sc, sc2tog; rep from * to end. (18 sts)

Rnd 18: *1sc in next sc, sc2tog; rep from * to end. (12 sts)

Stuff firmly.

Rnd 19: Sc2tog around. (6 sts)

Cut yarn, leaving a long tail. Thread through rem sts and pull tight to close.

ELENA

Using MC and 1.75mm (size 6) hook, make 6sc in magic circle.

Rnd 1: 2sc in each sc. (12 sts)

Rnd 2: *1sc in next sc, 2sc in next sc; rep from * to end. (18 sts)

Rnd 3: *1sc in each of next 2 sc, 2sc in next sc; rep from * to end. (24 sts)

Rnds 4–7: 1sc in each sc. (24 sts)

Rnd 8: 1sc in back loop of each sc. (24 sts)

Change to CC.

Rnd 9: *1sc in each of next 3 sc, 2sc in next sc; rep from * to end. (30 sts)

Rnds 10–14: 1sc in each sc. (30 sts)

Rnd 15: *1sc in each of next 3 sc, sc2tog; rep from * to end. (24 sts)

Rnd 16: *1sc in each of next 2 sc, sc2tog; rep from * to end. (18 sts)

Rnd 17: *1sc in next sc, sc2tog; rep from * to end. (12 sts)

Stuff firmly.

Rnd 18: Sc2tog around. (6 sts)

Cut yarn, leaving a long tail. Thread through rem sts and pull tight to close.

EKATERINA

Using MC and 2.0mm (size 4) hook, make 6sc in magic circle.

Rnd 1: 2sc in each sc. (12 sts)

Rnd 2: *1sc in next sc, 2sc in next sc; rep from * to end. (18 sts)

Rnd 3: *1sc in each of next 2 sc, 2sc in next sc; rep from * to end. (24 sts)

Rnds 4–8: 1sc in each sc. (24 sts)

Rnd 9: 1sc in back loop of each sc. (24 sts)

Change to CC.

Rnd 10: *1sc in each of next 3 sc, 2sc in next sc; rep from * to end. (30 sts)

Rnds 11–12: 1sc in each sc. (30 sts)

Rnd 13: *1sc in each of next 4 sc, 2sc in next sc; rep from * to end. (36 sts)

Rnds 14–15: 1sc in each sc. (36 sts)

Rnd 16: *1sc in each of next 4 sc, sc2tog; rep from * to end. (30 sts)

Rnd 17: *1sc in each of next 3 sc, sc2tog; rep from * to end. (24 sts)

Rnd 18: *1sc in each of next 2 sc, sc2tog; rep from * to end. (18 sts)

Rnd 19: *1sc in next sc, sc2tog; rep from * to end. (12 sts)

Stuff firmly.

Rnd 20: Sc2tog around. (6 sts)

Cut yarn, leaving a long tail. Thread through rem sts and pull tight to close.

Make sure you embroider lots of pretty flowers on my dress.

SHAWL (ALL DOLLS)

Using MC, holding piece upside down and working into front loops, start in 13th st from the beg of Round 8 (Round 9 for Ekaterina), 2sc in next st, 2hdc in each of next 2 sts, 2dc in each of next 2 sts, 2tr in each of next 14 sts, 2dc in each of next 2 sts, 2hdc in each of next 2 sts, 2sc in next st.

Fasten off.

FINISHING

Cut short length of MC and tie through two front sc of shawl to make a bow.

Cut circle from cream felt for face. Cut hair shape from yellow felt and stick to top of face with adhesive. Using blue embroidery floss, embroider French knots for eyes. Using pink embroidery floss, work back stitch for mouth. Using a cotton swab, apply powder blush to cheeks in small circles. Stick face to front of head.

Cut dress panel shape from cream felt. Embroider flowers in lazy daisy stitch using blue, green, and pink embroidery floss and work back stitch in green for the vines. Stick dress panel to front of dress, fitting under front of shawl.

Note: All three dolls are made in continuous spiral rounds, so you will not join with a slip stitch. Use a stitch marker throughout to mark the first stitch of each round.

Hello Ekaterina! I'm all dressed up and ready to go.

Tiny Flowers Bracelet

This simple pattern can be customized to suit your style with different colors or flower placement, or even by adding beading or sequins. It's just perfect for spring, or when you just want to feel springlike!

FLOWER (MAKE 8)
Using A, ch4, join with ss to form a ring.

Rnd 1: Ch1, make 10sc in ring, ss in first sc to close.

Rnd 2: *Ch2, 1hdc in same st, 1hdc in next st, ch2, ss in same st, ss in next st; rep from * to end.

Fasten off, leaving a long tail for sewing.

BRACELET BAND
Using B, ch51.

Row 1: 1sc in second ch from hook and each ch across, turn. (50 sts)

Rows 2–5: Ch1, 1sc in each sc across, turn.

At the end of Row 5, ss across short end of band to center, ch6, then ss in same place as last ss to form button loop.

Fasten off.

FINISHING
Weave in all ends except one long end on each flower for sewing.

Sew button to non-loop end of bracelet band. Sew flowers to band in desired placement.

Make the flowers in colors to match your favorite outfit.

SIZES
Flower: ⅞ in. diameter
Bracelet: 7 in. long

ABBREVIATIONS
ch(s): chain, chains
hdc: half double crochet
rep: repeat
Rnd: round
sc: single crochet
ss: slip stitch
st(s): stitch, stitches

MATERIALS
- Small amounts of No.5 crochet cotton, such as DMC Petra No.5 100% cotton, in various colors (A)
- Oddment of No.5 crochet cotton, such as DMC Petra No.5 100% cotton, in green (B)
- 1.5mm (size 8) steel crochet hook
- Sewing needle
- 1 x ½-in. diameter button

Itty-bitty Snowflake Garland

Let it snow, let it snow, let it snow! During the festive season, this pretty garland is the perfect touch for bookshelves, doorways, or even a spot on the tree. Make it as long as you like by adding more snowflakes. It crochets up quickly and easily, and the fuzzy mohair makes a beautiful halo around each flake.

SIZES
Each snowflake: 1¼ in. diameter

ABBREVIATIONS
ch(s): chain, chains
hdc: half double crochet
rep: repeat
Rnd: round
sc: single crochet
sp: space
ss: slip stitch

MATERIALS
- ¼ x ball, approx 57 yds, of laceweight yarn, such Rowan Kidsilk Haze 70% mohair/30% silk, in white
- 1.5mm (size 8) steel crochet hook

SNOWFLAKE
Ch4, join with ss to form a ring.
Rnd 1: *Ch5, [1hdc in ring, ch3] 6 times, join with ss in second ch of first ch-5.
Rnd 2: [2sc, ch4, 2sc] in each ch-3 sp, join with ss in first sc.
  Ch14, join with ss in fourth ch from hook to form ring for next snowflake; rep from * until garland is desired length.

FINISHING
Weave in ends.

Notes: One 25g ball of laceweight yarn will be enough to make a sizable garland—the sample shown used less than ¼ of a ball. You could add more chains between each of the snowflakes if you prefer to have a longer garland.

Snowman and Bauble Cover

Decorative delights for the festive season—Mr Snowman can also easily be transformed into an ornament by running a loop of ribbon through his head. The bauble cover was made for a 2½-in. diameter bauble, but could be made for any size bauble by increasing in any round.

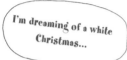

I'm dreaming of a white Christmas...

SNOWMAN
BODY

Using A and 2.0mm (size 4) hook, make 6sc in magic circle, pull tail to close.
Rnd 1: 2sc in each sc. (12 sts)
Rnd 2: 2sc in each sc. (24 sts)
Rnd 3: *1sc in next sc, 2sc in next sc; rep from * to end. (36 sts)
Rnds 4–13: 1sc in each sc. (36 sts)
Rnd 14: *1sc in each of next 4 sc, sc2tog; rep from * to end. (30 sts)
Rnd 15: *1sc in each of next 3 sc, sc2tog; rep from * to end. (24 sts)
Rnd 16: *1sc in each of next 2 sc, sc2tog; rep from * to end. (18 sts)
    Fasten off.

HEAD

Using A and 2.0mm (size 4) hook, make 6sc in magic circle, pull tail to close.
Rnd 1: 2sc in each sc. (12 sts)

SIZES
Snowman: 2⅜ in. tall
Bauble: 2½ in. diameter

ABBREVIATIONS
cont: continue
ch(s): chain, chains
dc: double crochet
dc2tog: double crochet 2 together decrease. *Yo, insert hook into first st, yo, pull through a loop, yo and pull yarn through first two loops on hook. Without finishing st, rep from * into next st. Yo and pull yarn through all three loops on hook
rep: repeat
Rnd(s): round, rounds
sc: single crochet
sc2tog: single crochet 2 together decrease. Insert hook in next st, yo, pull through a loop. Without finishing st, insert hook in next st, yo and pull through a loop. Yo and pull through all three loops on hook

sp: space
ss: slip stitch
st(s): stitch, stitches
tr: treble crochet
tr2tog: treble crochet 2 together decrease. *Yo twice, insert hook into first st, yo, pull through a loop, [yo and pull through two loops on hook] twice. Without finishing st, rep from * into next st. Yo and pull yarn through all three loops on hook
yo: yarn over hook

MATERIALS
Snowman
- ½ x ball, approx 48 yds, of 4-ply baby yarn, such as Debbie Bliss Baby Cashmerino 50% cashmere/50% merino, in white (A)
- 2.0mm (size 4) steel crochet hook
- 5 x ¼ in. (6mm) safety eyes
- Toy stuffing
- Sewing needle

Hat and scarf
- Small amount of DK-weight cotton yarn in black (B)
- Small amount of DK-weight wool in red (C)
- 2.5mm (size 2) steel crochet hook
- Sewing needle

Carrot nose
- Small amount of 6-strand cotton embroidery floss divided into 3 strands, in orange (D)
- 1.5mm (size 8) steel crochet hook
- Sewing needle

Bauble cover
- Small amount of No.5 crochet cotton, such as DMC Petra No.5 100% cotton, in white (E)
- 1.5mm (size 8) steel crochet hook

Rnd 2: *1sc in next sc, 2sc in next sc; rep from * to end. (18 sts)

Rnd 3: *1sc in each of next 2 sc, 2sc in next sc; rep from * to end. (24 sts)

Rnd 4: *1sc in each of next 3 sc, 2sc in next sc; rep from * to end. (30 sts)

Rnds 5–8: 1sc in each sc. (30 sts)

Rnd 9: *1sc in each of next 3 sc, sc2tog; rep from * to end. (24 sts)

Rnd 10: *1sc in each of next 2 sc, sc2tog; rep from * to end. (18 sts)

Fasten off, leaving a long tail.

HAT

Using B and 2.5mm (size 2) hook, make 6sc in magic circle, pull tail to close.

Rnd 1: 2sc in each sc. (12 sts)

Rnd 2: *1sc in next sc, 2sc in next sc; rep from * to end. (18 sts)

Rnd 3: 1sc in back loop of each sc.

Rnds 4–7: 1sc in each sc.

Rnd 8: 2sc in front loop of each sc. (36 sts)

Fasten off.

SCARF

Using C and 2.5mm (size 2) hook, ch41, skip 1 ch, ss in next ch, 1sc in each ch to last ch, ss in last ch. Fasten off.

SCARF END BALLS (MAKE 2)

Using C and 2.5mm (size 2) hook, make 6sc in magic circle, pull tail to close.

Rnd 1: 1sc in each sc. (6 sts)

Fasten off, leaving a long tail.

CARROT NOSE

Using D and 1.5mm (size 8) hook, make 4sc in magic circle, pull tail to close.

Rnds 1–2: 1sc in each sc.

Fasten off, leaving a long tail.

FINISHING

Insert safety eyes in snowman head and secure. Insert safety eyes as buttons down the front of body. Stuff head and body firmly. Sew head to body. Sew nose to head.

Push each end of scarf into a scarf end ball and sew in place.

BAUBLE COVER

Using E and 1.5mm (size 8) hook, ch4, join with a ss in first ch to form a ring.

Rnd 1: Ch5, [1dc in ring, ch2] 5 times, join with a ss in third of first ch-5.

Rnd 2: Ss in first ch-2 sp, ch3, 2dc in same sp, *ch2, 3dc in next sp; rep from * to end, ch2, join with a ss in top of first ch-3.

Rnd 3: Ch4, skip 1 dc, 1tr in next dc, *ch3, 1dc in ch-2 sp, ch3, tr2tog in first and third dc; rep from * to end, ch3, 1dc in ch-2 sp, ch3, join with a ss in top of first dc.

Rnd 4: Ch3, *4dc in next ch-3 sp, ch1; rep from * to end, ss in top of first ch-3.

Rnd 5: Ss in next st, ch2, 1dc in next st, dc2tog in next 2 dc, *ch2, [dc2tog in next 2 dc] twice; rep from * to end, ch2, join with a ss in top of first dc.

Insert bauble after this round and cont crocheting around bauble.

Rnd 6: Ch2, 1dc in dc2tog, ch3, *dc2tog in next two dc2tog, ch3; rep from * to end, join with a ss in top of first dc.

Rnd 7: Ch1, *ch3, 1sc in top of dc2tog; rep from * to end, join with a ss in top of first ch.

Rnd 8: Ss in next ch-3 sp, *ch1, [1sc, ch3, 1sc] all in same sp; rep in each sp from * to end, ch1, join with a ss in first sc.

Fasten off.

Easter Eggs and Baby Chick

Tufty the chick is waiting for his brother and sisters to hatch. He keeps asking his mom, Henny Pen, when they'll come out of their colorful shells. In the meantime, he likes to spend lots of time with the eggs, talking to them and playing them music.

EGG

Using A, make 6sc in magic circle.

Rnd 1: 2sc in each sc. (12 sts)

Rnd 2: *1sc in next sc, 2sc in next sc; rep from * to end. (18 sts)

Rnds 3–7: 1sc in each sc. (18 sts)

Rnd 8: *1sc in next sc, sc2tog; rep from * to end. (12 sts)

Rnds 9–10: 1sc in each sc. (12 sts)

Stuff firmly.

Rnd 11: *1sc in next sc, sc2tog; rep from * to end. (8 sts)

Fasten off, leaving a long tail.

CHICK

BODY

Follow egg pattern, using B. Insert safety eyes and secure after Round 10.

WINGS (MAKE 2)

Using B, make 6sc in magic circle.

Pull tail to make half-moon shape.

Fasten off, leaving a long tail.

FEET

Using orange, [ch4, skip first ch, 1sc in next 3 chs, ss in same ch as last sc] twice.

Fasten off, leaving a long tail.

FINISHING

Close hole in top of eggs and chick body using yarn end. Sew wings and feet to chick body. Cut small triangle of orange felt and stick to chick face to form beak. Cut short lengths of B and pull through top of chick head, then unravel to form a tuft.

> If you don't hatch soon, you'll miss all the chocolate.

SIZES

Egg: 1⅜ in. tall

Chick: 1½ in. tall

ABBREVIATIONS

ch(s): chain, chains

rep: repeat

Rnd(s): round, rounds

sc: single crochet

sc2tog: single crochet 2 together decrease. Insert hook in next st, yo, pull through a loop. Without finishing st, insert hook in next st, yo and pull through a loop. Yo and pull through all three loops on hook

ss: slip stitch

st(s): stitch, stitches

yo: yarn over hook

MATERIALS

Eggs

• Small amounts of 4-ply baby yarn, such as Patons Fairytale Dreamtime 4-ply 100% wool, in pink, blue and white (A)

• 2.0mm (size 4) steel crochet hook

• Toy stuffing

• Sewing needle

Chick

• Small amount of 4-ply baby yarn, such as Patons Fairytale Dreamtime 4-ply 100% wool, in yellow (B)

• 2.0mm (size 4) steel crochet hook

• 1 x pair ¼ in. (6mm) safety eyes

• Toy stuffing

• Small amount of DK cotton, such as Patons Linen Touch 74% cotton/24% linen, in orange

• Sewing needle

• Small piece of orange felt

• Craft/fabric adhesive

Note: For striped egg, alternate colors every two rounds. For half-and-half egg, change color after round 5. For 3-band egg, change color after round 2 and again after round 7.

Tiny Bead Bracelet

This pretty bracelet can be made in pastels, as shown, for a soft look, or bright colors for more of a kick. The bracelet shown is made with nine beads, but you can make as many as desired for a longer or shorter length. You could even make a matching necklace by making more beads and threading them in the same way.

BEAD (MAKE 2 IN EACH COLOR)
Make 6sc in magic circle, pull tail to close.
Rnd 1: 2sc in each sc. (12 sts)
Rnds 2–4: 1sc in each sc. (12 sts)
   Stuff firmly.
Rnd 5: Sc2tog around. (6 sts)
   Cut yarn, leaving a long tail. Thread through rem sts and pull tight to close.

FINISHING
String beads onto a length of crochet cotton, tying a knot between each (use sewing needle to keep knot close to bead while tightening). Tie into a bow, or attach two halves of a jewelry clasp if desired.

Note: The beads are made in continuous spirals, so you will not join with a slip stitch. Use a stitch marker throughout to mark the first stitch of each round.

SIZES
Bead: about ⅝ in. diameter
Bracelet: 6 in. (excluding ties)

ABBREVIATIONS
rem: remaining
Rnd(s): round, rounds
sc: single crochet
sc2tog: single crochet 2 together decrease. Insert hook in next st, yo, pull through a loop. Without finishing st, insert hook in next st, yo and pull through a loop. Yo and pull through all three loops on hook

st(s): stitch, stitches
yo: yarn over hook

MATERIALS
- Oddments of No.5 crochet cotton, such as DMC Petra Perle No.5 100% cotton, in three colors
- 1.5mm (size 8) steel crochet hook
- Toy stuffing
- Sewing needle
- Jewelry clasp (optional)

Make the beads in colors to match your favorite outfit.

Four-leaf Clover Keychain

Bring the luck of the Irish to all your friends—this clever four-leaf clover is quick and easy to make, making it the perfect last-minute gift for any friend who loses keys.

CLOVER LEAVES (MAKE 8 HALVES)

Row 1: Ch3, skip 1 ch, 1sc in each of next 2 chs, turn. (2 sts)

Row 2: Ch1, 1sc in each sc, turn.

Row 3: Ch1, 2sc in each of next 2 sc, turn. (4 sts)

Row 4: Ch1, 1sc in each sc, turn.

Row 5: Ch1, 2sc in next sc, 1sc in each of next 2 sc, 2sc in last sc, turn. (6 sts)

Row 6: Ch1, 1sc in each sc, turn.

Row 7: Ch1, [1sc, 1hdc] in next sc, [1dc, 1hdc] in next sc, ss in next sc, [1hdc, 1dc] in next sc, [1hdc, 1sc] in next sc, ss in last sc.

Fasten off, leaving a long tail.

STEM

Ch11, skip 1 ch, 1sc in next 10 sc.

Fasten off, leaving a long tail.

FINISHING

Use yarn end to sew two halves of a leaf together with whip stitch, stuffing lightly before closing final side. Rep for rem three leaves. Sew base of all four leaves together in clover shape.

Sew stem to clover, then sew keychain finding to back of clover. Sew button to middle of clover, if desired.

SIZE

1¼ in. across

ABBREVIATIONS

ch(s): chain, chains

dc: double crochet

hdc: half double crochet

rem: remaining

rep: repeat

sc: single crochet

ss: slip stitch

st(s): stitch, stitches

MATERIALS

- Small amount of No.5 crochet cotton, such as DMC Petra 100% cotton, in green
- 1.5mm (size 8) steel crochet hook
- Sewing needle
- Toy stuffing
- Keychain finding
- Small button (optional)
- Sewing needle

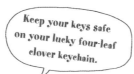

Keep your keys safe on your lucky four-leaf clover keychain.

Sweet Gingerbread Cottage

Can you imagine who lives inside this tiny cottage? Perhaps it's a family of ladybugs, or honeybees. Whoever it is, they like to keep things looking neat as a pin, with lots of colorful roof tiles and well-maintained topiary bushes in the front garden.

Anybody seen Hansel and Gretel?

SIZE
Cottage: 1¾ in. tall, 2 in. across eave to eave
Topiary bushes: 1 in. tall

ABBREVIATIONS
ch(s): chain, chains
dc: double crochet
hdc: half double crochet
rep: repeat
Rnd(s): round, rounds
sc: single crochet
sc2tog: single crochet 2 together decrease. Insert hook in next st, yo, pull through a loop. Without finishing st, insert hook in next st, yo and pull through a loop. Yo and pull through all three loops on hook
ss: slip stitch
st(s): stitch, stitches
yo: yarn over hook

MATERIALS
- Small amount of No.5 crochet cotton, such as DMC Petra No.5 100% cotton, in pink (A)
- Oddments of No.5 crochet cotton, such as DMC Petra No.5 100% cotton, in white (B) green (C), yellow (D), blue (E), and peach (F).
- 1.5mm (size 8) steel crochet hook
- Toy stuffing
- Oddments of 6-strand cotton embroidery floss in gray and pink
- Sewing needle

COTTAGE
FRONT AND BACK (MAKE 2)
Using A, ch11.
Row 1: Skip first ch, 1sc in each ch to end, turn. (10 sts)
Rows 2–10: Ch1, 1sc in each sc to end, turn.
Rows 11–13: Ch1, sc2tog, 1sc in each sc to last 2 sts, sc2tog, turn.
Row 14: Ch1, [sc2tog] twice, turn.
Row 15: Ch1, sc2tog.
   Fasten off.

SIDES AND BASE (MAKE 3)
Using A, ch11.
Row 1: Skip first ch, 1sc in each ch to end, turn. (10 sts)
Rows 2–10: Ch1, 1sc in each sc to end, turn.
   Fasten off.

ROOF (MAKE 2)
Using B, ch11.
Row 1: Skip first ch, 1sc in each ch to end, turn. (10 sts)
Rows 2–9: Ch1, 1sc in each sc to end, turn.
Row 10: Ch3, 2dc in same st, skip 1 st, ss in next st, skip 1 st, 5dc in next st, skip 1 st, ss in next st, skip 1 st, 3dc in last st.
   Fasten off.

ROOF TILES (MAKE 2 IN EACH COLOR)
Using C, D, E or F, ch11.
Row 1: Skip 2 chs, 2hdc in next ch, skip 1 ch, ss in next ch, skip 1 ch, 5hdc in next ch, skip 1 ch, ss in next ch, skip 1 ch, 3hdc in last ch.
   Fasten off, leaving a long tail for sewing.

WINDOWS (MAKE 2)
Using B, ch3.
Row 1: Skip first ch, 1sc in next 2 chs, turn. (2 sts)
Row 2: Ch1, 1sc in each of next 2 sc.
   Fasten off, leaving a long tail for sewing.

DOOR

Using B, ch4.

Row 1: Skip first ch, 1sc in each of next 3 chs, turn. (3 sts)

Rows 2–4: Ch1, 1sc in each sc across, turn.

Fasten off, leaving a long tail for sewing.

FINISHING

Join all the cottage wall pieces together with sc. Stuff cottage firmly and attach roof with sc. Sew tiles to roof, overlapping each layer slightly.

Use gray embroidery floss to stitch window detail. Sew windows to front of cottage.

Make a French knot in pink embroidery floss for doorknob. Sew door to front of cottage.

TOPIARY BUSHES (MAKE 2, OR MORE)

POT

Using F, ch2.

Rnd 1: 6sc in 2nd ch from hook.

Rnd 2: 2sc in each sc. (12 sts)

Rnd 3: 1sc in back loop of each sc. (12 sts)

Rnds 4–5: 1sc in each sc, ss in last sc to close. (12 sts)

Rnd 6: Ch2, 1hdc in each sc, ss to close.

Fasten off.

BUSH

Using C, make 6sc in magic circle. Pull tail to close.

Rnd 1: 2sc in each sc. (12 sts)

Rnd 2: *1sc in next sc, 2sc in next sc; rep from * to end. (18 sts)

Rnds 3–5: 1sc in each sc. (18 sts)

Rnd 6: *1sc in next sc, sc2tog; rep from * to end. (12 sts)

Stuff firmly.

Rnd 7: Sc2tog around. (6 sts)

Fasten off, leaving a long tail.

FINISHING

Use tail to close hole in bush, stitch bush to top of pot.

CHAPTER 5

Tiny friends

Who can resist smiling Dante the Dolphin, Annabelle the Doll with her own removable dress, or teeny weeny spotted ladybugs complete with a leaf to sit on? You will love to make stripey Stanley the Snail—easily created with self-striping yarn—or beautiful colorful fish in their own fishing net. Use fine artistic wire to curve Clive the Fuzzy Caterpillar into a distinctive shape, and don't forget the leaf accessories!

Tropical Fish and Starfish with Net

Colorfully striped tropical fish and a bright starfish are suspended in their own 'fishing net', a neat drawstring bag that can be used in many other ways.

TROPICAL FISH HEAD/BODY

Using first color and 1.0mm (size 12) hook, make 6sc in magic circle.

Pull tail to close.

Rnd 1: 2sc in each sc. (12 sts)

Rnd 2: *1sc in next sc, 2sc in next sc; rep from * to end. (18 sts)

Rnds 3–7: 1sc in each sc. (18 sts)

Change to second color.

Rnds 8–9: 1sc in each sc. (18 sts)

Change to first color.

Rnds 10–11: 1sc in each sc. (18 sts)

Change to second color.

Rnds 12–13: 1sc in each sc. (18 sts)

Change to first color.

Rnd 14: *1sc in next sc, sc2tog; rep from * to end. (12 sts)

Rnd 15: 1sc in each sc. (12 sts)

Stuff lightly.

Rnd 16: Sc2tog around. (6 sts)

Fasten off.

Is it a bird? Is it a plane? No, it's a starfish.

SIZES
Fish: 1½ in. long
Starfish: 1¾ in. across

ABBREVIATIONS
ch(s): chain, chains
foll: following
rep: repeat
Rnd(s): round, rounds
sc: single crochet
sc2tog: single crochet 2 together decrease. Insert hook in next st, yo, pull through a loop. Without finishing st, insert hook in next st, yo and pull through a loop. Yo and pull through all three loops on hook
sp: space
ss: slip stitch
st(s): stitch, stitches
yo: yarn over hook

MATERIALS
Tropical fish and starfish
- Small amount of No.8 crochet cotton, such as Rubi Perle No.8 100% cotton, in assorted colors
- Small amount of No.5 crochet cotton, such as DMC Petra No.5 100% cotton, in white (A)
- Small amount of No.8 crochet cotton, such as Rubi Perle No.8 100% cotton, in orange (B)
- 1.0mm (size 12) and 1.5mm (size 8) steel crochet hooks
- Toy stuffing
- Black embroidery floss
- Sewing needle

Fishing net
- ⅛ x ball, approx 104m, of No.5 crochet cotton, such as Anchor Artiste No.5 100% cotton, in beige (E)
- 2.5mm (size 2) steel crochet hook

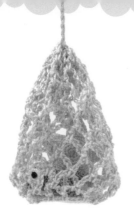

TAIL (MAKE 2)

Using second color and 1.0mm (size 12) hook, make 6sc in magic circle, pull tail to close.

Rnd 1: 2sc in each sc. (12 sts)

Rnd 2: 1sc in each sc. (12 sts)

Rnd 3: Sc2tog to 3 sts.

Fasten off, leaving a long tail.

EYE WHITES (MAKE 2)

Using A and 1.5mm (size 8) hook, make 8sc in magic circle, pull tail to close.

Fasten off, leaving a long tail.

STARFISH (MAKE 2)

Using B and 1.0mm (size 12) hook, make 6sc in magic circle, pull tail to close.

Rnd 1: 2sc in each sc. (12 sts)

Rnd 2: *1sc in next sc, 2sc in next sc; rep from * to end. (18 sts)

Rnd 3: *1sc in each of next 2 sc, 2sc in next sc; rep from * to end. (24 sts)

Rnd 4: *1sc in each of next 3 sc, 2sc in next sc; rep from * to end. (30 sts)

Row 1 of arm: Without cutting yarn, ch1, 1sc in each of next 6 sc, turn.

Row 2: Ch1, 1sc in each of 6 sc, turn. (6 sts)

Row 3: Ch1, sc2tog, 1sc in each of next 2 sc, sc2tog, turn. (4 sts)

Row 4: Ch1, 1sc in each of next 4 sc, turn.

Row 5: Ch1, [sc2tog] twice, turn. (2 sts)

Row 6: Ch1, 1sc in each of next 2 sc, turn.

Row 7: Ch1, sc2tog.

Fasten off.

Reattach yarn to work Rows 1–7 of arm on next 6 sts of rnd 4. Rep on foll 6 sts each time until all 5 arms are complete.

FISHING NET

Using E and 2.5mm (size 2) hook, ch4, join with ss to first ch to form a ring.

Rnd 1: 12sc into ring.

Rnd 2: *1sc in next sc, 2sc in next sc; rep from * to end. (18 sts)

Rnd 3: *1sc in each of next 2 sc, 2sc in next sc; rep from * to end. (24 sts)

Rnd 4: *1sc in each of next 3 sc, 2sc in next sc; rep from * to end. (30 sts)

Rnd 5: *1sc in each of next 4 sc, 2sc in next sc; rep from * to end. (36 sts)

Rnd 6: *1sc in each of next 5 sc, 2sc in next sc; rep from * to end. (42 sts)

Rnd 7: Ss in next sc, *ch6, miss 2 sc, 1sc in next sc; rep from * to end, ss in first 6-ch sp to join.

Rnds 8–15: *Ch6, 1sc in next ch-6 sp; rep from * ending ch6, miss 2 sts, 1sc in first ch-6 sp.

Ch60, fasten off.

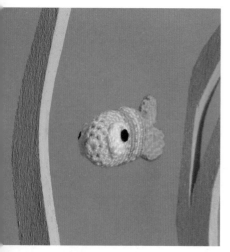

FINISHING

Sew both halves of fish tail to end of body.

Use black embroidery floss to embroider inner eye on eye whites. Sew eyes to fish.

Join two halves of starfish together with sc, stuffing lightly before joining second edge of final arm.

Weave length of ch through top of net and pull closed as a drawstring.

Dante the Dolphin

Splish splash! Dante the playful dolphin loves to frolic in the sea with his friends. He's always happy, as his smiling face shows.

Where's that sunbed—I can't wait to catch some rays!

HEAD AND BODY

Using A, make 6sc in magic circle, pull tail to close.

Rnd 1: 2sc in each sc. (12 sts)

Rnd 2: *1sc in next sc, 2sc in next sc; rep from * to end. (18 sts)

Rnd 3: *1sc in each of next 2 sc, 2sc in next sc; rep from * to end. (24 sts)

Rnds 4–6: 1sc in each sc. (24 sts)

Rnd 7: *1sc in each of next 3 sc, 2sc in next sc; rep from * to end. (30 sts)

Rnds 8–10: 1sc in each sc. (30 sts)

   Insert safety eyes and secure.

Rnd 11: *1sc in each of next 8 sc, sc2tog; rep from * to end. (27 sts)

Rnd 12: *1sc in each of next 7 sc, sc2tog; rep from * to end. (24 sts)

Rnd 13: *1sc in each of next 6 sc, sc2tog; rep from * to end. (21 sts)

Rnd 14: *1sc in each of next 5 sc, sc2tog; rep from * to end. (18 sts)

Rnd 15: *1sc in each of next 4 sc, sc2tog; rep from * to end. (15 sts)

Rnd 16: *1sc in each of next 3 sc, sc2tog; rep from * to end. (12 sts)

   Stuff firmly.

Rnd 17: *1sc in each of next 2 sc, sc2tog; rep from * to end. (9 sts)

Rnd 18: *1sc in next sc, sc2tog; rep from * to end. (6 sts)

Rnd 19: Sc2tog around. (3 sts)

   Fasten off, leaving a long tail.

SIDE FLIPPERS (MAKE 2)

Using A, make 4sc in magic circle, pull tail to close.

Rnd 1: *1sc in next sc, 2sc in next sc; rep from * once more. (6 sts)

Rnd 2: 2sc in each sc. (12 sts)

Rnds 3–5: 1sc in each sc. (12 sts)

Rnd 6: 1sc in next sc, sc2tog; rep from * to end. (8 sts)

   Fasten off, leaving a long tail.

SIZE
2 in. long, 1½ in. tall to top of fin

ABBREVIATIONS
ch(s): chain, chains
rep: repeat
Rnd(s): round, rounds
sc: single crochet
sc2tog: single crochet 2 together decrease. Insert hook in next st, yo, pull through a loop. Without finishing st, insert hook in next st, yo and pull through a loop. Yo and pull through all three loops on hook
sc3tog: single crochet 3 together decrease: *Insert hook into first st, yo, pull through a loop. Without finishing st, rep from * into each of next 2 sts. Yo and pull yarn through all four loops on hook
ss: slip stitch
st(s): stitch, stitches
yo: yarn over hook

MATERIALS
- Small amount of No.5 crochet cotton, such as DMC Petra No.5 100% cotton, in bright blue (A) and light blue (B)
- 1.5mm (size 8) steel crochet hook
- 1 x pair ¼ in. (6mm) safety eyes
- Toy stuffing
- Sewing needle
- Black embroidery floss

BACK FIN (MAKE 2 HALVES)

Using A, ch6.

Row 1: Miss 1 ch, 1sc in each of next 5 chs, turn. (5 sts)

Row 2: Ch1, 1sc in each sc, turn.

Row 3: Ch1, sc2tog, 1sc in next sc, sc2tog, turn. (3 sts)

Row 4: Ch1, sc3tog, turn.

Row 5: Ch1, 1sc in sc.

    Fasten off, leaving a long tail.

TAIL FINS (MAKE 2)

Using A, make 4sc in magic circle, pull tail to close

Rnd 1: *1sc in next sc, 2sc in next sc; rep from * once more. (6 sts)

Rnd 2: *1sc in next sc, 2sc in next sc; rep from * to end. (9 sts)

Rnd 3: 1sc in each sc. (9 sts)

    Ss in next sc and fasten off, leaving a long tail.

BELLY

Using B, ch8.

Rnd 1: Miss 1 ch, 3sc in next ch, 1sc in each of next 5 chs, 3sc in last ch. Working down other side of ch, 1sc in each of next 5 chs.

Rnd 2: *2sc in each of next 3 sc, 1sc in each of next 5 sc; rep from * once more.

Rnd 3: *[1sc in next sc, 2sc in next sc] 3 times, 1sc in each of next 5 sc; rep from * once more.

    Ss in next st and fasten off, leaving a long tail.

FINISHING

Use yarn end to close hole in body. Sew open edge of side flippers to sides of body.

Sew two halves of back fin together with whipstitch, stuffing lightly. Leave one long yarn end and use to sew fin to back of body.

Use yarn ends to sew open edge of tail fins to either side of point at end of body, as shown, and to sew belly to bottom of body.

Embroider mouth in black embroidery floss.

Annabelle the Doll

Annabelle is eight years old. She adores pretty dresses, but also loves climbing trees, so her mom is always having to mend her dresses and put adhesive bandages on scraped knees. Annabelle likes having long hair, even though she has to tie it back most of the time so she can go on her adventures.

HEAD AND BODY

Using A make 6sc in magic circle. Pull tail to close.

Rnd 1: 2sc in each sc. (12 sts)

Rnds 2–6: 1sc in each sc. (12 sts)

Rnd 7: Sc2tog around. (6 sts)

Rnd 8: 2sc in each sc. (12 sts)

Rnds 9–13: 1sc in each sc. (12 sts)

Stuff firmly.

Rnd 14: Sc2tog around. (6 sts)

Fasten off, leaving a long tail for sewing.

SIZE

3 in. tall

ABBREVIATIONS

ch(s): chain, chains

hdc: half double crochet

rep: repeat

Rnd(s): round, rounds

sc: single crochet

sc2tog: single crochet 2 together decrease. Insert hook in next st, yo, pull through a loop. Without finishing st, insert hook in next st, yo and pull through a loop. Yo and pull through all three loops on hook

ss: slip stitch

st(s): stitch, stitches

yo: yarn over hook

MATERIALS

Doll

- ¼ x ball, approx 27 yds, of DK cotton, such as Patons Linen Touch 74% cotton/24% linen, in pale beige (A)
- 2.0mm (size 4) steel crochet hook
- Toy stuffing
- Sewing needle
- Oddments of 6-strand embroidery floss in red and bright blue
- Small amount of No.5 crochet cotton, such as DMC Petra No.5 100% cotton, in yellow (D)

Dress

- Oddments of No.5 crochet cotton, such as DMC Petra No.5 100% cotton, in pink (B) and blue (C)
- 1.5mm (size 8) steel crochet hook
- Sewing needle

Hello! Don't forget the pretty bows in my lovely blonde hair.

ARMS AND LEGS (MAKE 4)

Using A, make 5sc in magic circle.

Rnds 1–3: 1sc in each sc.

Fasten off, leaving a long tail for sewing.

DRESS

Using B, ch21, join with ss into ring.

Rnds 1–4: Ch1, 1sc in each sc.

Change to C.

Rnd 5: Working in front loop only, *ss in next st, ch2; rep from * to end.

Rnd 6: Ch1, 1sc in back loop of sc from Round 4 around, ss in first sc to close.

Rnd 7: Ch2, 4hdc in same st, *miss 2 sts, 5hdc in next st (hdc cluster made); rep from * to end, ss in top of first ch-2.

Rnd 8: Ss to third st of first hdc cluster, ch2, 4hdc in same st, *5hdc in third st of next hdc cluster; rep from * to end, ss in top of first ch-2 to close.

Fasten off, weave in ends.

STRAPS FOR DRESS (MAKE 2)

Using B, ch11, miss first ch, 1sc in each ch.

Fasten off, leaving a long tail.

FINISHING

Use yarn end to close hole in doll. Embroider face on doll using red and bright blue embroidery floss. Sew arms and legs to body.

For hair, cut 6-in. lengths of D. Insert hook in top of head, fold one length of yarn in half over hook, and pull through to form a loop, then pull cut ends through loop. Trim to length when all hair has been inserted. Arrange hair in two bunches and tie with a length of bright blue embroidery floss.

Sew straps to dress bodice. Put dress on doll.

Make a selection of outfits in different colors.

Stanley the Snail

This little snail is remarkably easy to make, as the wool does all the work! There are many beautiful self-striping sock wools available—why not make a family of snails in several colorways?

Now where's that tasty leaf I was munching on earlier?

SIZE
Snail: 1⅛ in. tall
Leaf: 1¾ in. long

ABBREVIATIONS
ch(s): chain, chains
dc: double crochet
hdc: half double crochet
rep: repeat
Rnd(s): round, rounds
sc: single crochet
sc2tog: single crochet 2 together decrease. Insert hook in next st, yo, pull through a loop. Without finishing st, insert hook in next st, yo and pull through a loop. Yo and pull through all three loops on hook
ss: slip stitch
st(s): stitch, stitches
tr: treble crochet
yo: yarn over hook

MATERIALS
Snail
- Small amount of self-striping 4-ply sock wool, such as Rico Superba Mexico 75% Wool/25% Polyamide (A)
- 2.0mm (size 4) steel crochet hook
- 1 x pair ¼ in. (6mm) safety eyes
- Toy stuffing
- Sewing needle

Leaves
- Oddments of DK weight yarn in orange, gold and russet
- 2.0mm (size 4) steel crochet hook
- Sewing needle

SNAIL
BODY
Using A, make 6sc in magic circle, pull tail to close.
Rnd 1: 2sc in each sc. (12 sts)
Rnds 2–36: 1sc in each sc. (12 sts)
Insert safety eyes and secure. Stuff final 7 rounds only.
Rnd 37: Sc2tog around. (6 sts)
Fasten off, leaving a long tail.

ANTENNAE (MAKE 2)
Using A, ch7, miss 1 ch, 1sc in each of next 6 chs. (6 sts)
Fasten off, leaving a long tail.

FINISHING
Use yarn end to close hole in snail. Sew antennae to head.
Coil other end to form a shell and sew in place.

LEAF (MAKE 1 IN EACH COLOR)
Ch11, miss 1 ch, 1sc in next ch, *1hdc in next ch, 1dc in each of next 2 ch, 1tr in each of next 2 ch, 1dc in each of next 2 ch, 1hdc in next ch**, 3sc in last ch.
Working down other side of ch; rep from * to **, 2sc in last ch, ss in first sc.
Fasten off.

FINISHING
Weave in ends.

Note: You could make the leaves in several different shades of green, or in bright autumn colors as shown here.

Little Ladybugs

Alice and Edith have been friends since they both hatched from their tiny eggs. They like to spend time on the same leaf, munching on aphids and chatting about their ladybug adventures.

Note: You could also use the leaf with a crocheted flower to make a brooch, or sew several leaves to another crochet project as embellishment.

SIZES
Ladybug: ⅝ in. long
Leaf: 3 in. long

ABBREVIATIONS
ch(s): chain, chains
dc: double crochet
hdc: half double crochet
rep: repeat
Rnd: round
sc: single crochet
ss: slip stitch
st(s): stitch, stitches
tr: treble crochet

MATERIALS
Ladybugs
- Oddments of 6-strand cotton embroidery floss in red (A), black (B) and white (C)
- 1.5mm (size 8) steel crochet hook
- Sewing needle

Leaf
- Oddments of 4-ply cotton, such as Wendy Supreme 100% cotton 4-ply, in green (D)
- 2.0mm (size 4) steel crochet hook

LADYBUG
BODY
Using A, make 6sc into magic circle, pull tail to close.
Rnd 1: 2sc in each sc. (12 sts)
Rnds 2-3: 1sc in each sc. (12 sts)
Ss in first sc to join, cut yarn and fasten off.

BASE
Using B, ch5, miss first ch, 1sc in next ch, 1hdc in each of next 2 chs, 3sc in last ch.
Working down other side of ch, 1hdc in each of next 2 chs, 1sc in next ch.
Fasten off, leaving long tail for sewing.

FACE
Using B, make 4sc into magic circle, pull tail to close.
Rnd 1: 2sc in each sc. (8 sts)
Cut yarn, leaving a long tail for sewing.
Fasten off.

FINISHING
Tuck yarn ends inside body to act as stuffing. Sew base of ladybug to body with whip st.
Use B to embroider French knots as spots. Using C, embroider eyes on face. Sew face to front of body with whip st.

LEAF
Using D, ch22.
Rnd 1: Ss in second ch, *1hdc in each of next 4 chs, 1dc in each of next 4 chs, 1tr in each of next 4 chs, 1dc in each of next 4 chs, 1hdc in each of next 4 chs**, ss in same st as last hdc. Working down other side of ch; rep from * to **, join with ss in first ss.
Rnd 2: *1hdc in each of 4 hdc, 1dc in each of 4 dc, 2tr in each of 4 tr, 1dc in each of 4 dc, 1hdc in each of 4 hdc**, ss in ss; rep from * to **, join with ss in first ss.
Fasten off.

ladybug, ladybug, fly away home.

Fuzzy Caterpillar

Clive the fuzzy caterpillar spends all day on his leaf, munching slowly around the edges until he's had his fill. He's hoping to grow a few more segments, so he makes sure to eat as much as possible. Clive can be posed in a variety of positions thanks to the fine wire that runs through his segments.

CATERPILLAR SEGMENTS (MAKE 2 OR MORE IN EACH COLOR)
Make 6sc in magic circle, pull tail to close.
Rnd 1: 2sc in each sc. (12 sts)
Rnd 2: *1sc in next sc, 2sc in next sc; rep from * to end. (18 sts)
Rnds 3–5: 1sc in each sc. (18 sts)
Rnd 6: *1sc in next sc, sc2tog; rep from * to end. (12 sts)
 Turn so fuzzier side is facing out and stuff firmly.
Rnd 7: Sc2tog around. (6 sts)
 Cut yarn, leaving a long tail. Thread through rem sts and pull tight to close.

FINISHING
Thread all segments onto a length of yarn and secure. Fold a double length of wire in half and push through all segments, allowing the ends to form the antennae.

Note: Make the caterpillar longer for younger children to avoid any danger of choking. Do not add the wire if the caterpillar is for a younger child, as it may cause a scratch.

I'm not really a caterpillar–I'm a bookworm.

SIZE
Approx 2⅛ in. long

ABBREVIATIONS
rem: remaining
rep: repeat
Rnd(s): round, rounds
sc: single crochet
sc2tog: single crochet 2 together decrease. Insert hook in next st, yo, pull through a loop. Without finishing st, insert hook in next st, yo and pull through a loop. Yo and pull through all three loops on hook
st(s): stitch, stitches
yo: yarn over hook

MATERIALS
- Small amounts of laceweight yarn, such Rowan Kidsilk Haze 70% mohair/30% silk, in green and pink
- 1.5mm (size 8) steel crochet hook
- Toy stuffing
- Sewing needle
- Short length of fine craft wire (optional)

Basic Techniques

HOLDING THE HOOK

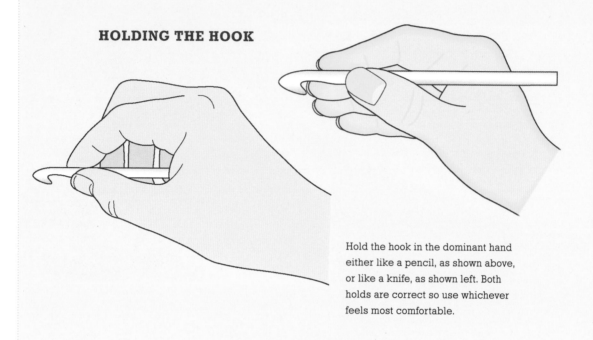

Hold the hook in the dominant hand either like a pencil, as shown above, or like a knife, as shown left. Both holds are correct so use whichever feels most comfortable.

HOLDING THE YARN

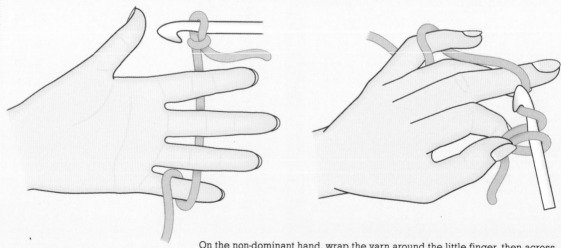

On the non-dominant hand, wrap the yarn around the little finger, then across the back of the other fingers—or take it over the palm side of the ring finger, and back of middle and first finger, whichever feels most comfortable.

Lift the middle finger to tension the yarn and hold the work with the first finger and thumb, as illustrated above right. Alternatively, lift the first finger to tension the yarn and hold the work with the middle finger and thumb.

MAGIC CIRCLE TECHNIQUE

This is also sometimes called magic/adjustable/slip ring or magic/adjustable loop.

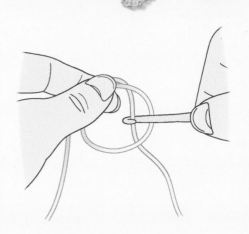

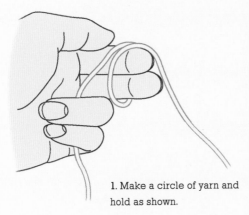

1. Make a circle of yarn and hold as shown.

2. Insert the hook into the circle, pull the active yarn through then make a chain.

3. Insert the hook into the circle (under both tail and circle side), yarn round hook and pull up a loop, yarn round hook again and pull through both loops on hook to make a single crochet.

4. Continue inserting the hook into the circle and make the required number of single crochet stitches.

5. Once you have made the required number of stitches, pull on the tail to close the circle (make sure the tail is free to pull and not wrapped round the circle).

MAKING A CHAIN (CH)

1. Start with a slip knot; make a loop in the yarn, insert the hook and catch the back strand.

2. Pull the yarn through to make a loop, then gently pull on both ends to close the loop on the hook.

3. Hold the slip knot with the non-dominant hand and push the hook forward and under the tensioned yarn, catching the yarn, then pull the yarn through the loop on the hook. One chain made.

SINGLE CROCHET (SC)

1. Insert the hook into the stitch or chain required. Yarn over hook and pull up a loop (2 loops on hook).

2. Yarn over hook again and pull through both loops on the hook. One single crochet made.

HALF DOUBLE CROCHET (HDC)

1. Yarn over hook first, then insert the hook into the stitch or chain required.

2. Yarn over hook and pull up a loop (3 loops on hook).

3. Yarn over hook and pull through all three loops on the hook. One half-double crochet made.

DOUBLE CROCHET (DC)

1. Yarn over hook first, then insert the hook into the stitch or chain required. Yarn over hook and pull up a loop (3 loops on hook).

2. Yarn over hook and pull through two loops on the hook (2 loops on hook).

3. Yarn over hook, pull through the last two loops on the hook. One double crochet made.

TREBLE (TR)

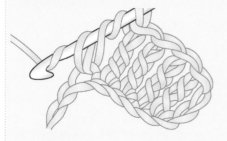

Yarn over hook twice first, then insert the hook into the stitch or chain required. Yarn over hook and pull up a loop, yarn over hook and pull through two loops, yarn over hook and pull through two loops again, yarn over hook and pull through the last two loops on the hook. One treble crochet made.

SINGLE CROCHET 2 TOGETHER (SC2TOG)

1. Insert the hook into the next stitch, yarn over hook, pull up a loop, then insert the hook into the next stitch.

2. Yarn over hook and pull up a loop, yarn over hook and pull through all three loops on the hook. One single crochet 2 together decrease made.

HALF DOUBLE 2 TOGETHER (HDC2TOG)

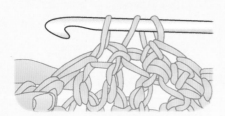

1. Yarn over hook, insert the hook into the next stitch, yarn over hook and pull up a loop (3 loops on hook).

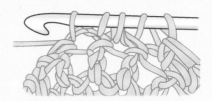

2. Yarn over hook, insert the hook into the next stitch, yarn over hook and pull up a loop (5 loops on hook).

3. Yarn over hook and pull through all five loops on the hook. One half-double 2 together decrease made. Double 2 together (dc2tog), is worked using the same basic technique (see page 21 for written instructions).

LOOP SINGLE CROCHET (LPSC)

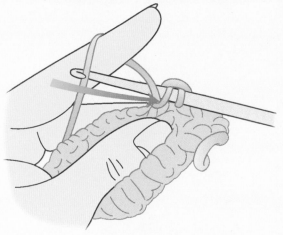

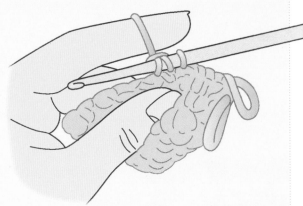

1. Insert the hook into the stitch required, yarn over hook with BOTH PIECES of yarn held over your tensioning finger, then pull through.

2. Adjust loop to the size desired, then finish the stitch. One loop single crochet stitch made.

YARN OVER (YO)

Also known as yarn round hook (yrh), or sometimes yarn over hook (yoh). The hook should always swing under the tensioned yarn, toward the back.

SLIP STITCH (SS)

Insert the hook into the stitch or chain required, yarn over hook and pull through both work AND loop on hook without making another yarn over. One slip stitch made.

FASTENING (FINISHING) OFF CROCHET

1. Cut the yarn, leaving a minimum 4 in. tail—leave longer for projects requiring a long tail.

2. Pull the tail all the way through the remaining loop on the hook to secure the end.

WORKING IN CONTINUOUS SPIRAL ROUNDS

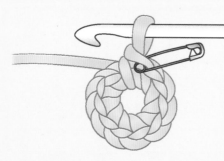

A chain is not necessary at the beginning of the round, and a slip stitch is not necessary at the end of the round. A new round will be started in the first stitch of the previous round. Use a stitch marker of some kind, such as a small safety pin as shown here, to mark the first stitch of the round.

WORKING INTO FRONT OR BACK LOOP OF STITCH

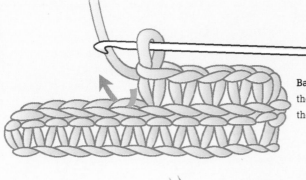

Back loop Insert the hook into only one leg of the V of the required stitch; the back loop is the leg further away from you.

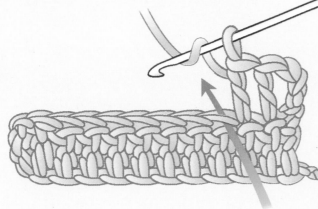

Front loop The front loop is the leg nearest to you.

Unless the pattern instructs you to use the front loop or the back loop, you should always insert your hook under both legs of the V of each stitch when crocheting.

AROUND THE POST STITCH

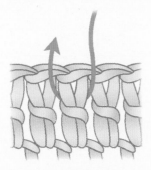

Front post stitch

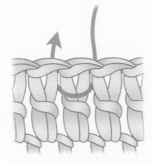

Back post stitch

Instead of inserting the hook into the V of the required stitch, insert it around the vertical part (the post) of the stitch from the row below.

SINGLE CROCHET JOIN

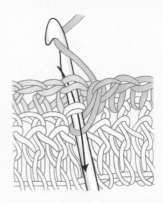

Insert the hook through both stitches to be joined, yarn over and pull up a loop, yarn over and pull through both loops on the hook.

Embroidery

FRENCH KNOTS

Bring the needle through to the front of work. Wrap the floss around the needle once, twice or three times depending on the size of knot desired, then insert the needle back into the work, very close to the original spot. Pull the wraps tight so they rest against the surface of the work, then pull the needle through to the back.

BACK STITCH

Bring the needle through to the front of the work. Take the needle to the back of the work to make a stitch the length desired (usually ¼ in.), then go forward a stitch length and bring the yarn through to the front of the work again. Go back to the end of the first stitch made and take the needle to the back. Repeat as required.

LAZY DAISY STITCH

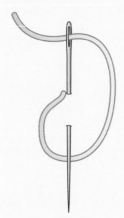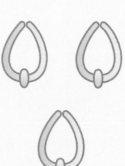

Bring the needle to the front of the work. Insert it into the same hole and, in the same motion, bring the needle back out a petal-length away and loop the floss around the tip. Take the needle to the back of the work on the other side of the loop, securing it, and bring back out in the center. Continue around in a circle until a daisy is made.

Useful Websites

DMC
www.dmc.com

COATS CRAFT
www.coatsandclark.com

PURL SOHO
www.purlsoho.com

ROWAN YARNS
www.knitrowan.com

PATONS
www.patonsyarns.com

DEBBIE BLISS
www.debbieblissonline.com

KNITTING GARDEN
www.theknittinggarden.com

MICHAELS
www.michaels.com

YARN MARKET
www.yarnmarket.com

YARN TREE
www.yarntree.com

YARNSTICK
www.yarnstick.co.uk

PARAGUAY THREADS
www.paraguaythreads.com

CATHERINE HIRST
www.catherinehirst.com

Acknowledgments

I am so grateful to everyone who helped make this book possible. Cindy Richards and Gillian Haslam at CICO Books made this project happen and were incredibly kind to me; thank you both. Many thanks to my fab editor Marie Clayton for being eagle-eyed and patient. Trina Dalziel created the beautiful sets for photography and Geoff Dann took the brilliant photos; thank you both for your vision. My beloved late grandmother, Catherine Jane, taught me to crochet when I was seven years old, which was the greatest gift she could have given me. Finally, I want to thank my husband Julian for his infinite patience, support, encouragement, and love.

Index